Casserole Crazy

Casserole Crazy

Hot Stuff
for Your
Oven!

Emily Farris

HOME

A HOME BOOK

Published by the Penguin Group

Penguin Group (USA) Inc.

375 Hudson Street, New York, New York 10014, USA

Penguin Group (Canada), 90 Eglinton Avenue East, Suite 700, Toronto, Ontario M4P 2Y3, Canada (a division of Pearson Penguin Canada Inc.) • Penguin Books Ltd., 80 Strand, London WC2R ORL, England • Penguin Group Ireland, 25 St. Stephen's Green, Dublin 2, Ireland (a division of Penguin Books Ltd.) • Penguin Group (Australia), 250 Camberwell Road, Camberwell, Victoria 3124, Australia (a division of Pearson Australia Group Pty. Ltd.) • Penguin Books India Pvt. Ltd., 11 Community Centre, Panchsheel Park, New Delhi—110 017, India • Penguin Group (NZ), 67 Apollo Drive, Rosedale, North Shore 0632, New Zealand (a division of Pearson New Zealand Ltd.) • Penguin Books (South Africa) (Pty.) Ltd., 24 Sturdee Avenue, Rosebank, Johannesburg 2196, South Africa

Penguin Books Ltd., Registered Offices: 80 Strand, London WC2R ORL, England

While the author has made every effort to provide accurate telephone numbers and Internet addresses at the time of publication, neither the publisher nor the author assumes any responsibility for errors, or for changes that occur after publication. Further, the publisher does not have any control over and does not assume any responsibility for author or third-party websites or their content.

Paula Deen's Crab and Spinach Casserole (page 86) originally appeared in *Paula Deen Celebrates!* by Paula Deen with Martha Nesbit (Simon & Schuster, 2006) and is reprinted with the permission of Simon & Schuster.

Copyright © 2008 by Emily Farris
Cover art and design by Ben Gibson
Text design by Richard Oriolo

First edition: October 2008

Library of Congress Cataloging-in-Publication Data

Farris, Emily
  Casserole crazy : hot stuff for your oven! / Emily Farris.— 1st ed.
    p.   cm.
  Includes index.
  ISBN 978-1-55788-535-7
  1. Casserole cookery.   2. Baking.   I. Title.
  TX693.F197 2008
  641.8'21—dc22   2008028670

PRINTED IN THE UNITED STATES OF AMERICA

10 9 8 7 6 5 4 3 2 1

PUBLISHER'S NOTE: The recipes contained in this book are to be followed exactly as written. The publisher is not responsible for your specific health or allergy needs that may require medical supervision. The publisher is not responsible for any adverse reactions to the recipes contained in this book.

Most Home books are available at special quantity discounts for bulk purchases for sales promotions, premiums, fundraising, or educational use. Special books, or book excerpts, can also be created to fit specific needs. For details, write: Special Markets, Penguin Group (USA) Inc., 375 Hudson Street, New York, New York 10014.

For Jo

Contents

Main Dishes

Macaroni and Cheese

Stove Top 171

Foreword

by JULIE POWELL, author of *Julie & Julia*

I met Emily for the first time at a reading in Williamsburg, Brooklyn. She came up to me at the bar before I was to go on, complimented me on the electric blue heels I had used my rare foray into this nationally recognized Zone of Hipness as an excuse to wear, and offered to buy me a vodka gimlet. I instantly knew three things: (1) this is a woman of both taste and daring; (2) though I am generally confused and/or irritated by women of taste and daring, I somehow am quite charmed by this young woman with the adorable red hair; and (3) she will be buying me that drink.

What I didn't catch quite as immediately was that this was also a chick who could throw together a mean casserole. I think it may have been the context that threw me off the scent at first. Williamsburg, Brooklyn, for those who don't know, is not a place one generally associates with comfort food. You can ironically drink Pabst Blue Ribbon in your ironically worn wifebeater until the cows come home, but finding a tuna casserole like Mom used to make (well, depending on your mom of course—my mom was actually a master at King Ranch Chicken, which is the Texas casserole of choice) is a job of work. In fact, you pretty much have to make it yourself: which is where Emily comes in.

When she tells the story of how we met, Emily will claim that she stalked me. Don't you believe it. What Emily did was connect me. She is a connector of people. All kinds of people. And as it turns out, casseroles are one of the essential tools of her trade.

By the end of the evening, she had convinced me, a party-phobe and generally misanthropic personality, to join her and a hundred of her closest friends for her birthday celebration the following week. At that surprisingly enjoyable party and in the time since, I've met many of Emily's friends—political activists, kickball players, and untold bloggers among them, plus one amateur burlesque dancer and professional knitter whom Emily met on the subway after she—the pro-knitter, I mean—had just bailed on a date she'd found through www.seekingarrangement .com. And often I've met these friends while eating casserole—a smorgasbord of casseroles, five or six in a night sometimes, all served in the incommodious kitchen of Emily's apartment, which would rate as "cozy" on Craig'sList, for sure. As one of those rare birds, the New York City apartment cook, I already knew that a home-cooked meal could bring together the friends and family you have; what Emily taught me with her Mac and Corn, Beet and Potato au Gratin, and

Grown-Up Tuna Noodle casseroles was that food could also introduce people as strangers and leave them sated friends.

But that's really what casseroles are all about, when you come down to it. Think church socials and firehouse fund-raising dinners, all those Midwestern traditions that seem—in Brooklyn, anyway—an unreal remnant of a Rockwellian past few of us ever really experienced.

It's a funny thing about casseroles. They're so simple, just a few diverse ingredients bound up into one delicious dish. That binder, be it stock or cream sauce or, my favorite, lots of gooey cheese, is what makes the casserole so inviting, and so communal. Casseroles can be wrapped, carried, reheated. Casseroles are for sharing, not just with the people you are comfortable with (or maybe stuck with) at your dinner table, but with folks you might not have met before you both dipped spoons into the same disposable tin pan laid out on the long tables of the community rec center.

So I guess, in my now-tortured metaphor, Emily is the gooey cheese. Not only does she bring people together with her food but she also brings together whole regions. Not content to rely solely on the comfort-food strengths of her Missouri roots, she looks to the hip, the ethnic, the sophisticated streets of New York for inspiration. The results are brighter, lighter dishes bursting with surprising flavors and wit. They're like what would happen if an Elk Lodge member and an amateur burlesque dancer met and hit it off famously. They are totally appropriate for digging into at the hippest Billyburg party around. You can even wash them down with your ironic PBR.

If you must.

I have only followed one recipe from start to finish in my life. It was on my twentieth birthday. I'd been in New York two years and wasn't much of a cook, as everyone in my family knew. In addition to my fear of knives, no one had ever taught me to prepare anything other than tricolor Rotini with butter and Parmesan, and I had never really cared to learn. But it was common knowledge that tuna noodle casserole was this Missouri girl's favorite thing in the entire world to eat. So on my birthday, when a giant box arrived in the mail from my aunt Susie, I was not at all disappointed to find everything I needed to make her famous tuna noodle casserole, including her secret ingredient, Salsa Con Queso Cheez Whiz, a can of French-fried onions, and a brand-new Pyrex dish, complete with a lid. She'd even sent a bottle of wine (very exciting for a twenty-year-old). Most important, however, was that she'd typed up and packed step-by-step instructions, including "Bring a medium pan of water to a boil (on top of the stove, not in the oven)." Though I knew that much, the directions were very helpful.

The next time I made the dish, I left out the Cheez Whiz and added extra white onion. Before long, I was a tuna-noodle-casserole-making machine, but I was adding my own special ingredients. While I loved Aunt Susie's classic tuna noodle, and always will, I was secretly testing my culinary capacity with Grown-Up Tuna Noodle—add artichoke hearts and freshly grated Parmesan cheese; hold the Cheez Whiz and French-fried onions.

And that's how this book was born—taking the tried-and-true recipes of my childhood, and giving them more spice, or sophistication. I've collected nearly fifty casserole cookbooks dating from 1920 to 1999, and I consult them often, usually for inspiration. I follow instructions until the halfway point and then decide I can do it better. Sometimes I can; other times it ends in complete disaster.

But looking at cookbooks, to me, is like looking through fashion magazines: I see combinations I wouldn't have thought up on my own or am inspired to try something crazy. Both give me a starting point. Both also give me ambition and direction. But, with both, I know that when it comes down to it, it's about what I can afford and what I love—not what someone tells me to love.

Sometimes I take the old recipes and just give them bacon or less butter. Other times, it's as simple as using a fresh sweet potato as opposed to canned. And with certain dishes nothing but a canned ingredient will do. But every once in a while, it's a little more complicated.

Casseroles for Everybody

I come from a meat-and-potatoes kind of place, where no one is allergic to anything (or so we like to tell them), and vegetarians are few and far between. Vegans might as well have purple faces and two noses. After moving to Brooklyn, and sharing the dinner table with vegans, vegetarians, and "lactards" (my friend Mike's term for people who are lactose intolerant, see "Lactard's Surprise" on page 128), I couldn't send out a dinner party invitation without asking for "dietary restrictions and preferences." It didn't take me long to realize that, while the culinary world may revolve around carnivores, the real world does not.

That's why I've done my best to include recipes for people with food allergies and those who wish to stay on the healthier side of life. After all, casseroles shouldn't *just* be a favorite of the fat and happy.

That said, this is a book for people who love to eat. It is not a book for people who like to make elaborate culinary presentations or impress dinner guests with knowledge of exotic vegetables or cuts of meat. This book is about taking ingredients that you know, that you love, that you can find, and baking those ingredients into one dish you can share with friends over an expensive bottle of wine or live off for a week when you're waiting for your next paycheck.

The History of the Casserole

The casserole as we know it today (e.g., tuna noodle, green bean, etc.) is a mixture of ingredients baked in one dish in the oven, or sometimes prepared on the stove. The self-contained meal has come a long way from the ancient practice of slowly stewing meat in earthenware—pottery-like clay containers.

The etymology of the word *casserole* can be traced back to the Greek term for cup, *kuathos*, progressing to the Latin word *cattia*, which could mean both "ladle" and "pan." *Cattia* became known in Old French as "casse," which then became *casserole*, and had variations like "cassoulet," a slow-cooked dish of white beans with pork, sausage, or duck, a meal that's still wildly popular in France.

As far as anyone knows, the word *casserole* was first used in the English language between 1706 and 1708, although it is believed the word wasn't used to describe more than the actual vessel for cooking until after World War I. This could have to do with the fact that Pyrex "glass dishes for baking" began to appear in America's hardware and department stores in 1915, offering home cooks nearly unbreakable cookware, in turn making casseroles more common in busy American households.

After the Great Depression and up until the end of World War II, one-dish meals that could be made on the cheap were a necessity for many families surviving on rations, canned goods, bread, and very little meat. Mixing dry bread crumbs with beef or chicken, broth, and a canned vegetable was a way to make a family's meat ration feed more people and last longer.

The casserole gained a different kind of popularity after the war, when new styles of fashionable cookware like lightweight Teflon and colorful Pyrex dishes hit department store shelves. Manufacturers of these products marketed the one-dish dinner as an easy and economical way to feed a family (and sell their cookware). Dishes were sold with miniature casserole cookbooks or recipe pamphlets with pictures of stylish women holding even more stylish cookware, and one-dish dinners were heavily promoted in women's magazines as a means to lighten the load of the 1950s housewife.

From 1960 to the early 1970s more women were joining the workforce, and the casserole, as we know it today, went from a clever, sensible way to feed a family to having a less-than-sophisticated reputation. In the late 1970s and '80s, while one-dish meals were widely accepted in other cuisines under the guise of "lasagna" and "noodle kugel," American-style casseroles were still being made with bland canned foods and bad cuts of meat. By the 1980s, the one-dish wonder was relegated to church basements and lower-to-middle-class Midwestern dinner tables like my own. By the late 1990s it had became the butt of many a foodie's joke. Oftentimes the word *casserole* garnered (and still garners) the following reactions:

"Ick!"

"Ugh!"

"Gross!"

"My mom used to make this one casserole when I was a kid and we had it all the time and I don't think I could bring myself to ever eat another one, ever!"

I've heard them all. And they're fair responses. People associate a bland tuna hot dish or creamy turkey concoction with "casserole" and they can't get those images out of their minds. If you allow yourself to think for a second about what a casserole really is, however, the possibilities are endless.

In addition to being time-saving and practical, casseroles are the perfect solution for the "domestically challenged." The beauty of a casserole, especially in its most basic form, is that by following a few simple guidelines you can throw your favorite ingredients in a casserole dish, pour some soup or broth over it, and stick it in the oven. Then, use that time to do something more important, like pour yourself a glass of wine and relax or catch up on those seventeen books you've been telling yourself and everyone else you're going to read.

In a slightly less simple form, there's some stove-top preparation and a few more pots and pans involved. In this scenario you should also pour yourself a glass of wine. But this is when you really begin to get away from the idea of casserole that's ingrained in your mind and experiment with fresh ingredients and new combinations like sweet potatoes and goat cheese; beets and gorgonzola; and zucchini with sweet corn and Parmesan.

If you're not yet convinced, to illustrate just how much casseroles have changed in recent years, I give you this paragraph from the introduction of *Casserole Treasury*, by Lousene Rousseau Brunner (Harper & Row, 1964):

> *A useful ingredient in practically all casserole dishes except desserts is monosodium glutamate (MSG), better known by such trade names as Accent. It is not listed here because it would appear in almost every recipe. I use it as I use salt and pepper. A little experimentation will provide a guide to quantities to use—it can go from a shake to a spoonful.*

You won't find any MSG here, kids. Just plain old salt and pepper. Use it. If you're feeling frisky, substitute sea salt and freshly ground pepper.

A Bad Rap, and a Party

I'll be the first to admit that because of ingredients like MSG and colorless, flavorless canned vegetables, the casserole has become synonymous with trailer parks, Milwaukee's Best, and contemporary country music. In fact, I once had a boyfriend (who was raised on both the West and East coasts) break up with me because I "make casseroles and sing bad karaoke."

So it's no wonder that I'd lived in New York four years before deciding to entertain with casseroles. I was sure my sophisticated, sushi-eating East Coast friends would pass over any Midwestern baked dish, leaving a Pyrex full of carbohydrates and fats for me to enjoy alone for the next week. But in the spring of 2004, I decided that the drunk brunch I was planning was the perfect time for the New York debut of my signature Mac and Corn Casserole, a recipe handed down from my older sister Heather and tweaked by me. It was a hit, and after a few experimental dinner parties—at which my tuna, macaroni, and green bean casseroles were devoured—I organized the First Annual Casserole Party.

The rules were strict and the competition was fierce. Sticking to my Midwestern idea of a casserole, each dish had to consist "of two or more solid ingredients (one is generally a noodle of some kind) . . . and baked in a casserole dish (generally known by the brand name Pyrex); cast iron will also be accepted." I threw the party on the cheap, only allowing teams of two with a casserole through the door. Little did I know how much everyone would love showing off their family favorites. (See Tips for Throwing Your Own Fabulous Casserole Party on page 181.)

The response was overwhelming. My apartment was packed, I gained five pounds, and the party was featured in the *New York Sun*. After the Second Annual Casserole Party, attendees and nonattendees alike were requesting that recipes be shared over email and my fellow Brooklynites were thanking me for adding a touch of "domestic bliss" to their hipster culture. Those who missed the party begged me to throw another the following month.

By the time the Third Annual Casserole Party rolled around, I had so many entries, I had to move it to a local restaurant, and because I was already hard at work on this book and on the lookout for new, exciting recipes, I eased up on the rules somewhat (layering was permitted) but I only allowed original or family recipes (some of which are included in these pages):

> Your "casserole" must fit the following criteria: An entrée consisting of two or more solid ingredients (one is generally a starch of some kind) BAKED in a casserole dish (generally known by the brand name Pyrex). Cast iron will also be accepted . . .

And that's where my definition of casserole has settled: two or more solid ingredients baked together in a casserole dish (though you'll see I do throw in a few stove-top casseroles at the end of the book, just to shake things up a bit).

Mixing It Up

The Food Encyclopedia, by Jacques Rolland and Carol Sherman (Robert Rose Inc., 2006), defines the casserole as "any of a wide variety of foods cooked in the same dish they're served in, containing meat, vegetables, rice, pasta beans or whatever the cook wishes to add."

And do I ever like to add. Gruyère and onions, mostly. But I'm still just a girl from Missouri with no formal culinary training and a constant hankering for tuna noodle casserole and anything with cheese. That's why, in addition to bringing you my own favorite original and family recipes, I've enlisted the help of people who know far more about food than I do. Their recipes far surpass my Parmesan cheese and sautéed onion quick fixes (which I hope you'll also enjoy).

Bobby Flay and restaurateur Donatella Arpaia offer up Italian-themed recipes, while Paula Deen, Ron Silver, Matt Hamilton, and Scott Gold ("The Shameless Carnivore") take American comfort food beyond its plain and simple roots. Katy Sparks offers up a fresh cauliflower gratin, and Alex Ureña makes paella seem almost easy.

With their recipes and mine, I hope there's something in this cookbook for everyone. Try the ones that seem appealing. And maybe even a few that don't. Add or remove an ingredient or two. Get your dishes dirty. The Pyrex dish Aunt Susie sent me now has permanent brown edges. I call that baked-on stuff "love" and like to think it gives my casseroles extra flavor.

The Basics

Brand Names

I have a very special relationship with Cascadian Farm frozen sweet peas. I have been known to go to four or five different bodegas in search of them when preparing a casserole. An old boyfriend rolled his eyes every time I called them "the good peas," until one night when we were dining in Red Hook, Brooklyn. As soon as I took a bite of my sweet mushroom risotto, I got far too excited because I was sure they'd used "the good peas." The boyfriend, who was a great cook in his own right but liked to think he knew more about food than he really did, rolled his eyes and told me that no company had the monopoly on "good peas" and that there was no way I could taste the difference.

In my ongoing effort to prove I was right about the things I truly believed in (and damnit, I believed in these peas), I asked our server if he knew where the restaurant got theirs. He didn't, but offered to ask the chef. I heard him at the window, "Chef, where do you get your peas?" I knew by the look on the chef's face that she was slightly embarrassed to use frozen peas in her dishes, even though it was winter. I also knew I was right. "Cascadian Farm?" our server yelled.

"Cascadian Farm," she yelled back with a confused smile.

So, obviously, I love these peas. And Cascadian Farm frozen sweet corn.

I often use Imagine soups and broths when I'm cooking for friends, because certain flavors are gluten-free or low in sodium.

Does it mean you can't substitute these brands for others? Absolutely not. These are just my suggestions, and if you have a brand you love or you can't find these, any old frozen peas will do. But please, for the love of all things green, don't use canned peas. (Sorry, Aunt Susie.)

Like I said, the casseroles you make are about what you like and what you can find, so don't go crazy trying to find the peas I use. Unless you're as crazy as I am. In that case, go get 'em, tiger.

On the Subject of Baking Time

The majority of the time spent writing this book, I lived in a run-down Brooklyn apartment with no oven knobs or counter space. After I had to emergency move out of that place because I could have harvested my own mushrooms from the bathroom ceiling and there were far too many creatures with far too many legs crawling around, I was in between apartments for a month and cooked in about ten different ovens. I quickly learned that cooking times vary by oven and can be dependent on the depth of your dish. So use the suggested times as a starting point. You'll know your casserole is ready when it's bubbly and crusty on top. And if you take it out and it's not done, stick it back in for a few minutes. This isn't steak we're dealing with here. Overcooking a casserole by a few minutes can't do much but make it a little crispier on top. And what's wrong with that?

On the Subject of Beans

Isn't the whole point of a casserole that it's supposed to be easy? This is why I don't bother with dried beans. Sure, I'll make you sauté onions and garlic—a lot—but I have never, nor will I ever, cook with dried beans when rinsed beans out of a can are just fine. That's why you won't find a cassoulet in this book. For the French-food purists, canned beans should never, ever be used in the dish. If you want to cook the recipes in this book with dried beans, it's up to you to figure out how to do it. And if you vastly improve upon one of my recipes by using dried beans, tell me about it at www.casserolecrazy.com. I like being shown up every once in a while.

One Large White Onion

I love onions. I love everything about onions. I even love that they make me cry (get out the psychology books). Onions make food taste better. That's why just about every casserole I make calls for one large white onion. Does this mean you must put one large white onion in every casserole you make from this book? Nope. If you don't like onions, I think you're weird (or seven years old), but don't use them. If you like them a little, use half an onion instead.

Let's Talk About Pasta

Mmm. Pasta. Pasta is good. Really, really good. Okay, now that that's settled, let's talk about cooking it, or parboiling it. For nearly every recipe in this book that requires pasta, I direct you to parboil it. That means undercook it. You're familiar with al dente, right? We're going for a little less cooked than that. If you fully cook your pasta, it can be overcooked and mushy after it's baked, depending on how much moisture is in the dish. If the box says, "Perfect in 9 minutes," six or seven is probably good. Egg noodles need about two to three in boiling water, and most semolina pastas will need more time than that. Taste it. If it's just a little too chewy, it's perfectly parboiled. But, you know, use your noodle.

Rice, Rice, Baby

I tend to use parboiled rice in my casseroles. It eliminates the step of precooking, and let's be honest: cooking rice without a rice cooker is a bitch. There aren't too many dishes in this book that call for rice, but in the ones that do, I get pretty specific about how to go about preparing it for each dish, and what kind of rice to use. Also, orzo can be a great rice substitute. Best of all, however, is getting cooked rice from the Chinese restaurant on the corner.

On the Subject of Dessert Casserole

While writing this book, people often asked if I would include dessert casseroles and my answer was always no. As far as I'm concerned, any dish that would qualify as a dessert casserole also qualifies as an already-established dessert like a cake, crumble, or pie.

Take Rice Krispies Treats, for example. By name it is already far more popular than something like Rice Krispies Casserole, because even if I were to add nuts and chocolate chips to the mix, I would still be making a pimped-out Rice Krispies Treat. (Plus you can't put onions in a dessert casserole, and by now you know how much I love onions.)

Composting

Over the past few years, I've been cooking at a much higher frequency and with fresher ingredients than I ever have. I found myself throwing out quite a bit of green waste (onion skins, potato peels, apple cores). Whenever the second half of an onion or half a bunch of carrots would go bad in my fridge, I started to feel guilty. And then I remembered something I'd learned many years ago in school: composting, or using broken-down organic material as a natural fertilizer. While I don't have a garden of my own to fertilize, there are plenty of parks and public green spaces in my area that do. So I started saving my green waste in a grocery bag in the freezer (that way it wouldn't stink!) and each week dropped it off at my local community garden. So if you don't know what to do with those leftover vegetables (and can't find a casserole in here that incorporates them), or you just feel bad about throwing your green waste in the trash, start composting. Find out if parks or gardens in your area are accepting compost, or use it in your own garden.

Go forth with your Pyrex, plenty of cheese, and a keen eye for a bubbly dinner. Don't be afraid to mix things up. Just don't forget the onions.

No matter what I eat for breakfast, I always mush it all into the same serving. Whether it's yogurt with berries and granola when I'm feeling like I should be healthy; eggs, bacon, and hash browns I pile high on my buttered whole wheat toast; or sausage, egg, and cheese on an everything bagel, breakfast foods just seem to all go well together—at the same time, in my mouth.

Maybe that's why I'm such a fan of the breakfast casserole, and its possibilities for classic mashed-up goodness—like sausage, egg, and cheese; asparagus and ham; and mushroom and cheese in a piecrust. I've also discovered some wonderful flavor combinations I wouldn't have thought would go well together in a breakfast casserole, like banana, apple, golden raisins, honey, cinnamon, and cheddar cheese, in the Capirotada, my take on a classic Mexican dessert.

Whether you perfect one of these recipes or attempt them all, remember that breakfast is the most important meal of the day—especially if you've been partying too hard the night before. And if breakfast is a casserole, it can be a whole day's worth of meals or a whole week's worth of breakfasts.

Most of these casseroles can be made ahead of time and refrigerated so there's very little work involved the next morning.

Sausage, Egg, and Cheese Casserole

FILE UNDER: Oh So Good but Bad for You

If you're as grumpy and/or hungover as I am most mornings, this super-easy breakfast casserole can and should be made the night before you plan to eat it. Whoever crashes on your couch will be beyond grateful to wake up to this, and you won't have to fight over who has to run out for bagels. This recipe will serve eight marginally hungry people, but if you're cooking for two, feel free to halve it. It's traditionally made without onions, so leave them out if you're so inclined.

SERVES 8

2 tablespoons olive oil

1/2 large white onion, finely chopped

1 pound pork or turkey sausage, crumbled

Cayenne pepper, optional

6 eggs

2 cups milk

Salt and pepper

6 slices white or whole wheat bread, cut or torn into 1/2-inch cubes

1 1/2 cups shredded cheddar cheese

Preheat oven to 350°F.

In a skillet over medium heat, sauté the onions in olive oil. When the onions are brown, add the sausage and cayenne pepper, if using. Drain and set aside.

In a large bowl, beat the eggs and milk. Salt and pepper to taste. Stir in the bread cubes, 1 cup of the cheese, and the sausage mixture. Pour into a buttered 2 1/2 to 3-quart baking dish.

(If you need to, cover and refrigerate for 8 hours or overnight. Remove from the refrigerator 30 minutes before baking.) Bake, uncovered, at 350°F for 45 minutes. Remove from oven and top with the remaining 1/2 cup cheddar cheese. Bake an additional 10 to 15 minutes.

Asparagus Breakfast Casserole

FILE UNDER: **Oh So Good but Bad for You**

This breakfast casserole, courtesy Bo Kersey, a family friend in Atlanta, is perfect for Sunday brunch. There's never a shortage of food when Bo and his partner, Jay, entertain, and dishes like this are the reason why. It's super simple to prepare and serves ten to twelve hungry people. It can be made ahead of time or the night before and refrigerated. **SERVES: 10 TO 12**

1½ pounds fresh asparagus, cut into 2-inch pieces

4 to 5 tablespoons butter, melted

1 loaf (1 pound) sliced bread with crusts or a baguette

1 cup shredded cheddar cheese, divided

2 cups cubed fully cooked ham, or bacon or cooked ground sausage

6 eggs

3 cups milk (it's great with half-and-half)

3 small green onions, green and white portions, minced

½ teaspoon salt

¼ teaspoon ground mustard

Preheat oven to 325°F.

In a saucepan, cook asparagus in water over medium-high heat until just tender but still firm. Drain and set aside.

Lightly brush butter over one side of each bread slice. Place half of the bread, buttered side up, in a greased 13×9×2-inch baking dish. Sprinkle with ½ cup of the cheese. Layer with the asparagus and ham. Cover with the remaining bread, buttered side up. (If you need to, at this point cover and refrigerate overnight. Let stand for 30 minutes before proceeding.)

In a bowl, lightly beat the eggs; add the milk, onions, salt, and mustard; pour over the bread. Bake, uncovered, for 50 minutes. Remove and sprinkle with the remaining cheese. Return to the oven for 10 minutes or until the cheese is melted and a knife inserted near the center comes out clean.

Breakfast Lasagna

Cathy Erway of "Not Eating Out in New York" really doesn't eat out. At all. At least not since she started her website (www.noteatingoutinny.com). She has cooked almost all of her meals herself, so she's always coming up with new dishes and combining ideas like breakfast and dinner in this lasagna with mushrooms, bacon, and cheddar.

This recipe uses fresh pasta made from flour and eggs, and rolled into flat lasagna sheets with a pasta crank. If you don't own a crank, you can try to roll the dough out as thin as possible with a well-floured rolling pin until you have roughly four square sheets, but you can also just buy the conventional lasagna sheets to use as a substitute. Cathy encourages substituting different cheeses or even vegetables for the cheddar and mushrooms, but I like it just the way it is.

SERVES 6 TO 8

1 cup all-purpose flour

9 eggs

1 cup milk

Salt and freshly ground black pepper

2 tablespoons butter

1 pound button mushrooms, trimmed and sliced

2 tablespoons fresh thyme

6 ounces sharp cheddar cheese, grated

3 slices bacon, cooked to crispy and crumbled

Put the flour in a wide, flat-bottomed bowl and create a well in the center. Crack 2 of the eggs into the center and mix up the yolks with your finger. While spinning the eggs with your finger, gradually bring in more flour from the edges of the well. Keep doing this until you have a workable dough to knead (add more flour if it sticks to your hands, or a spoonful at a time of water if it's so dry that it won't come together). Turn dough onto a floured, flat surface and knead for at least 10 minutes. Cover with plastic wrap and set aside for 15 minutes while you prepare the rest of the ingredients. When the dough is ready, cut it into three separate pieces and lightly flour each one before pressing it into thin pasta sheets following your pasta crank's directions.

Preheat oven to 375°F.

Beat together the remaining 7 eggs, the milk, and a pinch each of salt and pepper. Heat 1 tablespoon of butter in a pan and add the mushrooms and half of the thyme. Season with a pinch each of salt and pepper. Cook, stirring occasionally, for about 4 minutes, or until the mushrooms have cooked off most of their liquid.

Heavily grease the interior of a square 9×9-inch baking dish with the remaining butter. Pour about a third of the egg mixture into the bottom of the dish. Top with one even layer of the fresh pasta sheets (you may need to trim in order for them to fit nicely). Top the pasta with about a quarter of the shredded cheese. Top this with a third of the mushrooms, and a third of the bacon. Add another pasta layer. Slowly pour on top another third of the egg mixture, then top with another pasta layer. Top with a quarter of the cheese, and almost the rest of the mushrooms and bacon. Top with another pasta layer, another egg layer, and another pasta layer, or continue layering according to how many ingredients are left. On the very top of the casserole, sprinkle the remaining cheese, the rest of the thyme, and a little ground pepper.

Bake, uncovered, for about 30 minutes, or until top has lightly browned at its peaks.

Let stand at least 10 minutes before serving.

French Toast Casserole

FILE UNDER: Oh So Good but Bad for You, Vegetarian

This breakfast casserole is so easy it doesn't need to be prepared the night before, and is probably better fresh. It's certainly easier than standing over the stove making French toast for six people. Put it in the oven and cut up some fresh fruit to serve on the side. This goes great with mimosas, if you're cooking for the over-twenty-one crowd.   SERVES 5 TO 6

7 cups bread (white, wheat, or cinnamon-raisin) torn into 1½-inch cubes

1 tablespoons butter, softened

2 ounces cream cheese

1½ cups milk

4 eggs

¼ cup powdered sugar

¼ teaspoon salt

1½ teaspoons vanilla extract

1 teaspoon nutmeg

2 teaspoons ground cinnamon

Preheat oven to 350°F.

Line the bottom of a lightly buttered 9×9-inch casserole dish with the bread cubes.

In a large bowl, mix the butter and cream cheese. Add the milk and stir. Add eggs 1 at a time while continuing to stir. When mixed thoroughly, add 2 tablespoons of the sugar, the salt, the vanilla, the nutmeg, and 1 teaspoon of the cinnamon. Pour mixture over the bread. Let the casserole stand for 5 to 10 minutes so the liquid can soak into the bread.

Combine remaining sugar and cinnamon and sprinkle over the top.

Bake 45 to 50 minutes or until the top is golden brown.

Spinach Frittata

FILE UNDER: Not So Bad for You, Gluten-Free, Vegetarian

I was always afraid of making frittatas—anything that I am responsible for making rise is a little scary. But when I made this and realized how easy it was, I laughed at myself for not having attempted it before. While most people advocate serving frittatas at room temperature, I prefer mine warm. This simple spinach frittata calls for frozen spinach, but you can easily substitute fresh. If you can find good summer tomatoes where you are, I recommend adding a cup of chopped fresh tomatoes to the mix right before transferring it to the baking dish. But it's great without the tomatoes, too.

SERVES 6 TO 8

2 to 3 tablespoons olive oil

1 yellow onion, chopped

1 cup chopped baby portobello mushrooms

4 eggs

1 (10 ounce) package frozen chopped spinach, thawed and drained

1 cup ricotta cheese

1 cup freshly grated Parmesan cheese

1 pinch salt

Pepper to taste

1 teaspoon chopped fresh parsley, optional

1 cup chopped fresh tomatoes, optional

Preheat oven to 375°F.

In a pan over medium heat, sauté the onions and mushrooms in the olive oil until the onions become translucent. Remove from heat and set aside.

In a large bowl, mix the eggs, spinach, cheeses, salt, pepper, and parsley. Add the sautéed mushrooms and onions, and tomatoes if you're using them. Transfer entire mixture to a buttered 9-inch pie plate or 9-inch-square casserole dish.

Bake for 30 to 35 minutes, or until brown and set. You'll know it's set when it feels spongy. Let cool for 5 to 25 minutes, depending on whether you like your frittata warm or at room temperature.

Broccoli and Mushroom Quiche

FILE UNDER: **Not So Bad for You, Vegetarian**

This quiche is super-easy, especially if you use a premade piecrust (I prefer Pillsbury). Just remember to hide the crust packaging if you want your brunch guests to think you spent hours perfecting the crust. This recipe can easily be halved, as it makes two quiches (and it's okay to use 3 eggs if you halve it).   SERVES 10 TO 12

2 premade frozen piecrusts

5 eggs

¾ cup half-and-half or whole milk

Salt and pepper to taste

1 cup broccoli florets, lightly steamed

1 cup shredded cheddar cheese

1½ cups baby portobello mushrooms, chopped

Preheat oven to 400°F.

If using premade piecrusts, prepare according to directions for blind baking or let thaw for about 10 minutes, poke holes in them with a fork, and bake for 10 minutes or until golden. Set aside to cool.

In a large bowl, mix the eggs, milk, and pepper. When mixed thoroughly, add the broccoli, half the cheese, and salt. Mix well and then stir in the mushrooms. Divide the mixture evenly between the piecrusts. Top each evenly with the remaining cheese.

Bake, uncovered, 30 to 40 minutes or until quiche filling is set and the cheese on top is melted and beginning to brown.

Bacon, Egg, and Cheese Quiche

This savory breakfast quiche uses premade piecrusts (I prefer Pillsbury) and frozen pre-chopped spinach, so you can get away with looking like you did a lot more work than you actually did. But after you cook your bacon and before you crumble it, remember to blot the grease with a paper towel so your quiche isn't greasy. This recipe can be easily halved (and it's okay to use 3 eggs if you halve it). SERVES 10 TO 12

2 premade frozen piecrusts

5 eggs

3/4 cup half-and-half or whole milk

Salt and pepper to taste

1 (10 ounce) package frozen chopped spinach, thawed and drained

8 strips bacon, cooked and crumbled

1 cup shredded cheddar cheese

Preheat oven to 400°F.

If using premade piecrusts, prepare according to directions for blind baking, or let thaw for about 10 minutes, poke holes in them with a fork, and bake for 10 minutes or until golden. Set aside to cool.

In a large bowl, mix the eggs, milk, and pepper. When mixed thoroughly, add the spinach, bacon (save approximately 1/2 cup), half the cheese, and salt (you will need little to no salt because bacon is very salty). Pour mixture evenly into the piecrusts. Crumble remaining bacon over the top of each and sprinkle with the rest of the cheese.

Bake, uncovered, 30 to 35 minutes or until quiche filling is set and the cheese on top is melted and beginning to brown.

Capirotada Breakfast Casserole

FILE UNDER: Oh So Good but Bad for You, Vegetarian

My friend Jordana, whom I befriended after she wrote about my Second Annual Casserole Party for the *New York Post*, asked me to make a casserole for her with a Mexican theme. I started researching dishes, and was at first skeptical of the Capirotada, a baked Mexican dessert that sounded like a strange bread pudding. The idea of cheddar cheese, bananas, and cinnamon baked into the same dish was a little off-putting. But my appropriation makes it a great breakfast or brunch casserole, and the cheddar cheese adds an unexpected savory kick to the sweeter flavors of apple, banana, brown sugar, and golden raisins. A wonderfully surprising combination, after all.

SERVES 5 TO 7

1 cup honey

3 teaspoons cinnamon

1 cup raw pecans, chopped or crushed

1½ cups blanched, slivered, or sliced almonds

1 cup seedless golden raisins

1 teaspoon brown sugar

1 tablespoon butter

2 cups day-old bread or baguette (my preference), torn into 1-inch cubes

2 bananas, sliced

2 large green apples, peeled and chopped

½ pound sharp cheddar cheese, shredded

Preheat oven to 350°F.

Pour the honey into a heavy saucepan and bring to a light boil. (It will boil over like milk, so watch carefully.) Once boiling, add 2 teaspoons of the cinnamon, reduce the heat to low, and let it simmer, uncovered, for 5 to 7 minutes.

In a bowl, mix the pecans, almonds, and raisins with the remaining teaspoon of cinnamon and the brown sugar.

Butter the bottom of a 2-quart casserole dish and cover with half of the bread, then layer with half of the bananas, apples, nut mixture, and cheese. Repeat the layer in the same order using the remainder of these ingredients.

Pour the hot honey over the layered mixture in the dish (take it directly off the heat so it doesn't have time to harden).

Bake, uncovered, 30 to 35 minutes until the cheese has melted and the casserole is cooked through. It should be slightly brown on top when done.

Vegan Breakfast Casserole

FILE UNDER: **Not So Bad for You, Lactose-Free, Vegan, Vegetarian**
(can be made gluten-free if you use gluten-free soy sauce and tofu)

While I think just about everything is better with cheese, some things are great without it. This savory vegan breakfast casserole with potatoes, tofu, and broccoli is one of those things. The soy sauce and onion add bold flavor, while the cayenne and crushed red pepper add an unexpected kick to a combination of ingredients seen all too often in vegan breakfast dishes. As I was making this casserole my omnivorous roommate peered over the top of the mixing bowl and said, "I don't think I'm going to like this one." She did.

When I make vegan dishes, I tend to make them extra spicy to make up for the lack of fat. The spices I've indicated here are for flavor, not heat. So if you like spicy food, too, double the amount of cayenne and crushed red pepper, like I do.

TIP: Your potatoes will boil much quicker if you cut them before boiling (just be sure not to overcook them or they'll be mushy). Then you can strain them and run cold water over them to cool them off.   SERVES 6 TO 8

1½ large white onions, chopped

3 garlic cloves, minced or pressed

2 tablespoons olive oil

1 cup baby portobello mushrooms, cleaned and chopped

3 cups boiled potatoes, sliced

1 pound tofu, drained, mashed, and seasoned with salt and pepper

2 cups broccoli, steamed

3 tablespoons soy sauce

2 tablespoons chopped fresh parsley

2 teaspoons chopped fresh basil

½ teaspoon black pepper

½ teaspoon cayenne pepper

½ to 1 teaspoon salt

½ teaspoon crushed red pepper, optional

Preheat oven to 325°F.

In a large skillet over medium heat, sauté the onion and garlic in the oil until the onion becomes translucent. Add the mushrooms and sauté over low heat for an additional 5 minutes.

In a large bowl, mix together the potatoes, tofu, broccoli, soy sauce, and mushroom-onion mixture. Add the parsley, basil, black pepper, and cayenne. Add the salt and red pepper to taste. Transfer to a greased (Crisco is vegan!) 2½-quart baking dish, and bake, uncovered, for 40 to 45 minutes or until golden brown on top and hot throughout.

Potato and Egg Casserole

FILE UNDER: Oh So Good but Bad for You, Gluten-Free, Vegetarian

This breakfast casserole requires you to boil the potatoes ahead of time, so this is one you might want to make before you go out on Saturday night if you're planning to have it for Sunday brunch. You can easily add bacon to this recipe by cooking it with the garlic and onions and chopping it before it goes in the casserole. In this case, eliminate the olive oil, as the bacon grease will do the trick. SERVES 6 TO 7

2 pounds Yukon Gold potatoes, boiled, peeled, and sliced

2 to 3 tablespoons olive oil

2 large white onions, chopped

1 green bell pepper, chopped

4 cloves garlic, minced or pressed

6 large eggs

2 cups shredded cheddar cheese

2 cups heavy cream

1/2 cup fincly chopped chives

1/4 teaspoon cayenne pepper

1/2 teaspoon salt

Preheat oven to 350°F.

Layer the potatoes in a greased or buttered 9×13-inch baking dish.

In a skillet over medium heat, sauté the onions, green pepper, and garlic in the olive oil. Once the onions are translucent, pour over the potato slices.

In a mixing bowl, whisk together the eggs, cheddar, heavy cream, chives, cayenne, and salt. Pour mixture over the potatoes and onions.

Bake, uncovered, for about 45 minutes or until the eggs are set and slightly browned on top.

Spinach, Ham, and Mushroom Breakfast Casserole

FILE UNDER: **Not So Bad for You**

This casserole is so easy to prepare it doesn't need to be made the night before. If you do make it ahead of time, hold off pouring the egg mixture on top until you're ready to bake. Because this is a savory dish, I prefer to have it around noon with Bloody Marys to having it at 9 a.m. with orange juice. So sleep in and make it when you get around to it. Then eat it and go back to bed. Isn't that what Sundays are for?   SERVES 4 TO 5

3 cups of 1-inch bread cubes

1 cup fresh spinach, finely chopped

$1/2$ cup sliced baby portobello mushrooms

$1/2$ large white onion, finely chopped

8 ounces cubed or crumbled cooked ham, or sausage

1 cup shredded cheddar cheese

5 eggs, slightly beaten

$1^1/2$ cups milk

Salt and freshly ground pepper to taste

Preheat oven to 350°F.

Cover the bottom of a greased or buttered 8-inch-square casserole dish with half of the bread cubes. Cover with half of the spinach, mushrooms, onions, ham, and $1/4$ of the cheese. Layer with remaining bread cubes and repeat.

In a large bowl, mix the eggs, milk, half of the cheese, salt, and pepper. Pour the mixture over the casserole.

Bake, uncovered, 35 to 45 minutes or until cooked thoroughly.

In my book (and this is my book), two or more ingredients mixed and baked in the oven qualify as a casserole, so I had to include some of my favorite baked dips. While none is really a self-contained meal—because each requires some sort of edible dipping mechanism—I'd be remiss not to include some appetizer casseroles.

I often throw parties where I serve only dips. I'll offer up a spinach and artichoke dip with toasted white bread; an artichoke, sun-dried tomato, and bacon dip with warm whole grain bread; and a bean dip with fresh tortilla chips. Or, if I'm serving my Polish-themed "Greenpoint" casserole, I'll serve the kielbasa dip as an appetizer.

Preparing multiple dips takes very little work (because few involve stove-top prep), and cleaning up is even easier. I only have to wash the casserole dishes I baked the dips in and clean up all the bread crumbs.

Spicy Artichoke-Crab Dip

FILE UNDER: **Oh So Good but Bad for You, Gluten-Free**

My former roommate Amy Wu shared this recipe, after much begging on my part. Anytime she comes over and asks what she can bring, I always ask for this spicy artichoke-crab dip. It requires no stove-top preparation and goes best with tortilla chips or warm tortillas.

SERVES 6 TO 8 WITH CHIPS

1 (6 ounce) can crabmeat

1 (6.5 ounce) jar marinated artichoke hearts, lightly drained and chopped

10 slices pickled jalapeño, chopped

1½ cups mayonnaise

1 cup grated or shredded Parmesan cheese

1 tablespoon gluten-free seafood seasoning (such as Old Bay)

Paprika for garnish

Preheat oven to 375°F.

Mix the first 6 ingredients and pour into a 1½-quart ovenproof dish. Sprinkle with the paprika for garnish. Bake for 30 minutes until golden and bubbly.

Serve with tortilla chips or warm tortillas (just make sure you get gluten-free chips if you're going that route).

Spicy Black Bean Dip

FILE UNDER: **Not So Bad for You, Gluten-Free, Vegetarian**

This simple appetizer casserole requires no stove-top preparation and is great for parties. Make it as spicy or mild as you like. I really love onions, so I use a raw white onion, but if you prefer your onions softer, feel free to sauté them for a bit in a few tablespoons of olive oil before adding them to the dish. If you prefer jalapeños to cayenne, they go well in this dish and can be substituted.   SERVES 4 TO 6 WITH CHIPS

3 to 4 cloves of garlic, minced

1/2 large white onion, chopped

2 (15 ounce) cans black beans, rinsed

1 (16 ounce) can tomato sauce or pureed tomatoes

1 tablespoon olive oil

2 tablespoons cider vinegar

1 to 2 tablespoons cayenne pepper

1/2 tablespoon chili powder

Salt and pepper to taste

8 ounces cheddar cheese, shredded

1 to 2 jalapeño peppers, minced, optional

Preheat oven to 350°F.

In a large mixing bowl, combine the garlic, onions, beans, tomato sauce, olive oil, cider vinegar, and jalapeño, if using. Add the cayenne, chili powder, salt, and pepper. Continue to stir while adding half of the cheese.

Transfer to a 1½-quart baking dish and bake for 35 to 40 minutes.

Remove from oven and top with the rest of the cheese. Bake for an additional 10 minutes or until cheese is melted and the entire dip is bubbly.

Let stand 5 minutes before serving.

Grab some chips and dig in.

Beef, Black Bean, and Corn Dip

FILE UNDER: Oh So Good but Bad for You

This easy dip requires little stove-top preparation and is great for parties—especially Super Bowl parties with lots of hungry people, because this is a lot of food! Goes great with chips and beer. If you use a lean beef, there's no need to drain it after cooking.

SERVES 10 TO 12 WITH CHIPS

1 pound ground sirloin

1 tablespoon chili powder

$1/2$ teaspoon cayenne pepper

Salt and pepper to taste

1 large white onion, chopped

3 to 4 cloves of garlic, minced

2 (15 ounce) cans black beans, rinsed and drained

1 (28 ounce) can tomato sauce or pureed tomatoes

1 tablespoon olive oil

2 tablespoons cider vinegar

16 ounces frozen sweet corn

1 pound sharp cheddar cheese, shredded

Preheat oven to 350°F.

In a sauté pan over medium heat, cook the ground sirloin until brown. Season with the chili powder, cayenne, salt, and pepper. If you like your onions soft, you should cook them with the beef. If you like them crunchy, add them later.

In a large mixing bowl, combine the onions (if not already added), garlic, beans, tomato sauce, olive oil, and cider vinegar. Mix well. Add the beef, corn, and all but a handful of the cheese. Mix well and transfer to a $2^{1}/2$ to 3-quart baking dish and bake for 35 to 40 minutes or until bubbly. Remove and top with the remaining cheese and bake for an additional 5 to 10 minutes.

Let stand 5 minutes before serving.

Grab some chips and dig in.

Spinach-Artichoke Dip

FILE UNDER: Oh So Good but Bad for You or Not So Bad for You
(depending on whether you use low-fat ingredients),
Gluten-Free (if you're not dipping bread), Vegetarian

This dip requires no stove-top preparation and is always a hit. This particular recipe makes a ton. It's easily halved, but I make it for parties and it always goes quickly, especially if served with warm bread. This is a high-calorie dish, but if you use low-fat or fat-free mayonnaise and cream cheese, it's not so bad. If you choose to use low-fat ingredients, add an extra pinch or two (or seven!) of cayenne pepper for a little extra kick.

SERVES 8 TO 12 WITH CHUNKS OF WHOLE-GRAIN BREAD

2 (13.75 ounce) cans quartered artichoke hearts, roughly chopped

2 (10 ounce) packages frozen chopped spinach, thawed and drained

3 cloves garlic, minced

1/2 large white onion, chopped

16 ounces cream cheese, softened

1 cup mayonnaise

1 tablespoon dried basil

1 1/2 cups Parmesan and/or Romano cheese, grated

1/2 teaspoon cayenne pepper

Salt and pepper to taste

Cayenne pepper, optional

Preheat oven to 350°F.

Combine all ingredients in a large mixing bowl. Transfer to a 2 1/2 to 2 3/4-quart baking dish and bake, uncovered, for 45 minutes to an hour, depending on how deep your dish is. You'll know it's done when it's bubbly. I like to sprinkle a little of the Parmesan/Romano on top before I stick it in the oven. It will brown a little, and that's just fine.

Sun-Dried Tomato and Artichoke Dip

FILE UNDER: **Oh So Good but Bad for You or Not So Bad for You (depending on whether you use low-fat ingredients), Gluten-Free (if you're not dipping bread), Vegetarian**

This dip highlights two ingredients I wouldn't touch as a child and have grown to appreciate as an adult: sun-dried tomatoes and artichokes. It requires no stove-top preparation, but be sure to chop the sun-dried tomatoes and artichokes well to make for easy dipping. I use vacuum-packed sun-dried tomatoes because they don't need to be drained or rehydrated. Baking time will vary, depending on your oven and your dish. I like to cook this in a deep dish (a 2³/₄-quart square dish), so it takes longer to warm all the way through. Serve with chunks of warm whole-grain bread.

VARIATION: Add a few cups of crumbled bacon. Just be sure to blot the grease from the bacon before you crumble it or you'll end up with a very greasy dip.

SERVES 8 TO 12 WITH BREAD

2 (13.75 ounce) cans quartered artichoke hearts, chopped

12 ounces sun-dried tomatoes, finely chopped

3 cloves garlic, minced

¹/₂ large white onion, chopped

16 ounces cream cheese, softened

1 cup mayonnaise

1 tablespoon dried basil

1¹/₂ cups Parmesan and/or Romano cheese, grated

Salt and pepper to taste

Cayenne pepper to taste

1 teaspoon crushed red pepper

Preheat oven to 350°F.

Combine all ingredients (if you're using bacon, reserve a little to sprinkle on top when it's done) in a large mixing bowl. Transfer to a 2¹/₂ to 2³/₄-quart baking dish and bake, uncovered, for 45 minutes to an hour. You'll know it's done when it's bubbly and golden on top.

Spicy Curry Dip

FILE UNDER: Oh So Good but Bad for You, Vegetarian

This creamy dip with curry flavor is incredibly easy to prepare and can be made ahead of time, refrigerated, and heated when you're ready to eat it. If you're going to refrigerate it, let it stand at room temperature for 10 to 20 minutes so it doesn't burn on top. This is great for dipping toasted pita or fresh vegetables.   SERVES 6

1 cup sour cream

1 cup cream cheese

1 cup cottage cheese

1 tablespoon curry powder

$1/2$ teaspoon cayenne pepper

$1/2$ green bell pepper, finely chopped

Preheat oven to 350°F.

In a medium bowl, mix all the ingredients. Transfer to a $1\frac{1}{2}$ to 2-quart baking dish and bake, uncovered, for approximately 30 minutes.

Chili Queso Dip

FILE UNDER: Oh So Good but Bad for You

I have a confession to make: I love queso dip from a certain chain restaurant with a ridiculously catchy jingle. It's probably made with Velveeta cheese and Grade G beef, but I don't care—it's delicious. Especially when served with warm tortilla chips. This version is more beefy than cheesy but still delicious and spicy. And you can use real cheese.

SERVES 8 TO 10 WITH CHIPS OR TORTILLAS

1½ pounds lean ground beef

1 large white or yellow onion, chopped

1 green bell pepper, chopped

1 tablespoon chili powder

1 teaspoon cayenne pepper

Salt and pepper to taste

3 cups shredded sharp cheddar cheese

1 (28 ounce) can diced tomatoes, with juice

Preheat oven to 350°F.

In a pot or large saucepan over medium heat, brown the beef with the onion and bell pepper. When the beef is cooked through, add the chili powder, cayenne pepper, salt, and pepper. Add 2½ cups of the cheese, stirring until melted. When the cheese is melted, add the tomatoes and stir.

Transfer to a 2½-quart baking dish, cover with the remaining cheese, and bake 20 to 25 minutes or until the cheese begins to turn a golden brown.

Serve with tortilla chips.

Cheesy Corn Dip

FILE UNDER: Oh So Good but Bad for You, Gluten-Free, Vegetarian

The sharpness of cheddar paired with crispy sweet corn makes for a great crunchy dip. Cheddar cheese and corn go surprisingly well together, and the red bell pepper adds a splash of color to the dip. The cayenne pepper really brings out the flavor of the cheddar cheese.

SERVES 6

2 (16 ounce) bags frozen sweet corn

3 cups shredded sharp cheddar cheese

2 red bell peppers, finely chopped

1 large white or yellow onion, finely chopped

2 cups sour cream

$1/2$ teaspoon cayenne pepper

Salt and pepper to taste

Preheat oven to 350°F.

Mix all ingredients in a large bowl. Transfer to a 2 to $2^{1}/_{2}$-quart lightly greased baking dish and bake, uncovered, for 45 to 55 minutes or until bubbly.

Serve with corn chips.

Baked Kielbasa Dip

Cream cheese and browned kielbasa make a great combination for dipping corn chips or toasted bread. And if by chance you're hosting some kind of Polish-themed party, you can serve this before the Greenpoint (page 68). If your kielbasa released lots of grease, you should drain it from the pan or blot it with a paper towel to avoid a greasy dip. **SERVES 6 TO 8**

12 ounces kielbasa, chopped into $1/4$-inch pieces

$1/2$ large white onion, finely chopped

2 (8 ounce) packages cream cheese, softened

1 cup sour cream

6 tablespoons mayonnaise

1 cup Parmesan cheese

Preheat oven to 350°F.

In a pan or skillet over medium heat, sauté the kielbasa and onion until they begin to brown. Remove from heat.

In a large bowl, mix the cream cheese, sour cream, mayonnaise, and all but $1/4$ cup of the Parmesan cheese. Add the kielbasa and onion. Mix well, transfer to a 2-quart baking dish, and cover with the remainder of the Parmesan.

Bake, uncovered, for 30 to 40 minutes (depending on how deep your dish is) or until bubbly.

Layered Bean and Beef Dip

FILE UNDER: Oh So Good but Bad for You, Gluten-Free (as long as the taco seasoning is gluten-free)

This dip is a baked, mixed version of a layered Mexican dip. Once it comes out of the oven, top it with sour cream and fresh chives. As much as I hate to admit to liking a fast-food product found on grocery store shelves, Taco Bell refried beans are really, really tasty in this dish. But if you prefer another brand, by all means, go for it. **SERVES 8 TO 10**

1½ pounds lean ground beef

1 package taco seasoning

Salt and pepper to taste

¹⁄₂ teaspoon cayenne pepper

2 (15.5 ounce) cans refried beans

2 tablespoons diced jalapeños

1 large white onion, chopped

2 cups shredded cheddar cheese

1 cup sour cream

¹⁄₂ cup chopped chives

Preheat oven to 375°F.

In a large skillet over medium heat, cook the beef. When the beef is cooked, add the taco seasoning, salt, pepper, and cayenne. Remove from heat and let cool for a few minutes.

In a large bowl, mix the beef, beans, jalapeños, onions, and 1½ cups of the cheese.

Transfer to a greased 9×13-inch baking dish. Top with the remaining cheese and bake, covered, for about 20 minutes. Uncover and bake an additional 10 minutes or until cheese is melted and bubbly.

Remove from the oven and let stand 5 to 10 minutes. Top with sour cream and chives and serve with chips.

Casseroles grace dinner tables all over the world as side dishes, whether they're called casseroles or not. And if you grew up in the South or the Midwest, you know the side-dish casserole is the staple of the American potluck dinner. It's easily prepared, even easier to reheat, and is transported in the dish it's baked in (why else would Pyrex have handles?).

From variations on classic gratin dishes (of which there are many in this section, including Katy Sparks's Cauliflower Gratin) to baked rice dishes and kugels, you really can't get more American than baked starch.

In this section you'll find new takes on old favorites like Classic Green Bean Casserole and new dishes, like my Sweet Potato Not Pie, made with goat cheese, and my friend Kara Zuaro's French Onion Souperole.

Experiment with pairing the side dishes with a casserole from the main dish section. Or pair a side with a salad and a glass of wine and make a meal of it.

Sweet Potato Not Pie

FILE UNDER: Not So Bad for You, Gluten-Free, Vegetarian

The most ridiculous thing about this casserole is how easy it is. As it requires no stove-top preparation, a recipe is hardly necessary; you really just need six basic ingredients. This always goes before anything else I'm serving and will show up anyone's candied sweet potatoes at Thanksgiving. Also, if you like to drink while you cook, this recipe is nearly foolproof. Just don't forget to cover it when it goes in the oven or you'll end up with black sweet potatoes on top and raw ones on bottom. If you prefer a less spicy dish, use a bell pepper rather than a jalapeño or habañero pepper.

I've made this at least twenty times, but have never actually measured the olive oil. Sometimes there's a little extra in the bottom of the dish. Sometimes not.

VARIATION: Add ½ pound of cooked sweet sausage, sliced or crumbled. If you do this, use significantly less olive oil when creating the layers. SERVES 5 TO 6

5 to 6 medium sweet potatoes, peeled and thinly sliced

1 large white onion, chopped

1 green bell, habañero, or jalapeño pepper, thinly sliced

6 to 8 ounces fresh goat cheese, crumbled

¼ to ⅓ cup olive oil (you may not use it all)

Salt to taste

Preheat oven to 400°F.

Cover the bottom of a 2-quart casserole dish with a layer of sweet potatoes. Add a layer of onions, peppers, and goat cheese. Drizzle with a tablespoon of the olive oil and sprinkle with salt. Repeat layers until you reach the top of your dish (try to finish with sweet potatoes and just a drizzle of olive oil), saving at least 1 ounce of goat cheese for the end.

Cover and bake for 1 hour and 15 minutes to 1½ hours or until a fork goes through the entire dish easily. Remove from the oven and top with the remaining goat cheese. Bake, uncovered, for an additional 10 to 15 minutes.

Let stand for 10 minutes before serving.

Potato and Cauliflower Gratin

FILE UNDER: **Not So Bad for You, Gluten-Free, Vegetarian**

What this potato and cauliflower gratin lacks in color, it makes up for in flavor. An incredibly rich bake with cheese, cream, and butter, it's a great side for chicken or pork and should probably be served with a salad so you don't feel so guilty after eating it, even though it's not all that bad for you.   SERVES 5 TO 6

6 medium red potatoes, thinly sliced (about 6 cups)

1 head fresh cauliflower (about 4 cups)

4 tablespoons butter, softened

1 cup regular or light sour cream

¼ cup milk or cream

3 cloves garlic, minced or pressed

1 cup Parmesan cheese

1 large white onion, finely chopped

1 tablespoon chopped fresh parsley

¼ teaspoon cayenne pepper

Pinch salt and pepper

Preheat oven to 400°F.

Mix the potatoes and cauliflower in a 2½-quart baking dish. Mix the remaining ingredients in a medium bowl and pour over the casserole.

Bake, covered, for approximately 1 hour or until the potatoes are cooked through. For best results, remove from the oven and stir once while baking.

Mad's Butternut Squash Bake

FILE UNDER: **Not So Bad for You, Vegetarian (lactose-free and vegan if you skip the cheese)**

This butternut squash bake from my friend Kara Zuaro, author of *I Like Food, Food Tastes Good,* is the perfect example of a delicious dish made with simple ingredients. While the original recipe calls for Gorgonzola cheese, it can be left out for the vegans at your table.

This recipe was handed down from Kara's friend Madolyn Orr, a no-nonsense California cook, who describes it as a "healthy, hearty, full-flavored side dish." Both Kara and Madolyn encourage substitutions when necessary, or desired. For example, you can use dried cranberries instead of cherries, and walnuts or almonds instead of pecans.

SERVES 4

1/4 cup olive oil, plus enough to coat the casserole dish

1 butternut squash, peeled and cut into 1-inch pieces

1 red onion, roughly chopped

1/4 cup dried cherries

Salt to taste

Freshly ground pepper to taste

1/2 cup pecans

1/4 cup crumbled Gorgonzola cheese

Preheat oven to 425°F.

Put the butternut squash, red onion, and dried cherries in a greased 2-quart casserole dish, and drizzle with the olive oil. Sprinkle salt and freshly ground pepper over the casserole, and then toss the ingredients together.

Bake until the butternut squash is very soft and sweet. This will take 45 minutes to 1 hour, depending on the size of your squash. Every 10 minutes, shake the casserole dish to make sure the squash and onions aren't sticking to the sides (if they are, you can add some more olive oil), and prick the squash with a fork to test the doneness.

After about 40 minutes, the squash should be getting soft. Take the casserole out and stir in the pecans. At this point, you might want to taste the squash to make sure it's cooked through but not too soft; it's going back in the oven for a while and you don't want to overcook it. Take out a piece and be sure to let it cool off before you bite into it. Meanwhile, put the casserole back in the oven.

When the squash is perfectly soft (this will be sooner rather than later if your squash was already soft when you tasted it before) and the onions are beginning to brown, sprinkle the Gorgonzola over the dish, and put it back in the oven for just 1 or 2 minutes to melt the cheese. Then, take the casserole out, sprinkle with a little more salt and pepper, and enjoy—preferably with a glass of red wine from your favorite local vineyard.

French Onion Souperole

Another recipe from my friend Kara Zuaro, author of *I Like Food, Food Tastes Good*, this French Onion Souperole was created like so many casseroles before it—using leftover ingredients. Kara added day-old bread and fresh broth to the remains of a French onion soup (caramelized onions, cheese, and very little broth) and baked it. This recipe is a dressed-up version of that, and as Kara says, "It tasted like the love child of homey Thanksgiving stuffing and classic French bistro fare." She suggests using Pacific Natural Foods mushroom broth to keep this dish vegetarian friendly, but any flavorful broth will do.   SERVES 6

1 tablespoon butter	1 day-old baguette
1 teaspoon brown sugar	1 cup mushroom or beef broth
1/2 teaspoon salt	1 shot brandy
3 medium-size onions	2 teaspoons fresh thyme
1 tablespoon water	1/2 cup grated Swiss cheese
Freshly ground black pepper to taste	1/2 cup grated Fontina cheese
1 tablespoon olive oil	

Cut each onion in half and then into 1/4-inch slices.

Melt the butter in a large nonstick skillet over high heat, and then quickly stir in the sugar and salt. Add the onions, and stir to coat them in the butter mixture. The onions will be piled high at first, but they'll cook down to about a quarter of their original size. Stir the onions over high heat for about five minutes. Turn the heat down to medium.

Stir the onions frequently for the next 40 minutes or so. (Try to make the most of it. Crack open a beer and call up a faraway friend. Or crank up your favorite record from high school and meditate on how awesome it sounds and how cool you must have been for recognizing greatness in your teenage years.) If the onions start to burn, turn down the heat. If they haven't started to brown by the 20-minute mark, turn up the heat.

Once the onions are soft and brown, take them off the heat, add water, and grind some fresh pepper on top. If you're starting this recipe a day ahead, put the onions in the fridge after they've cooled, and do the rest tomorrow.

Preheat oven to 350°F and coat an 8×8-inch casserole dish with the olive oil.

Using a bread knife, cut the baguette lengthwise into quarters. Then, cut the 4 long strips into 1-inch slices. Ideally, you're using a slightly stale, day-old baguette, but if you've got a fresh one, put the pieces on a baking sheet and toast them for a few minutes in the oven as it heats up.

Measure the stock or broth in a liquid measuring cup, throw in a shot of brandy, and mix.

In a large bowl, toss together the baguette pieces, caramelized onions, and thyme. Pour the broth over the mixture, being careful to moisten all the bread evenly. Transfer the mixture to the casserole dish.

Top the casserole with a mixture of the grated Swiss and Fontina cheeses, and bake for 30 minutes, or until the cheese is melted and bubbly.

Kale and Parmesan Bake

Not So Bad for You, Vegetarian

Kale, a member of the cabbage family that more closely resembles spinach when cooked, is one of the most nutrient-packed green vegetables and is surprisingly delicious when sautéed with just olive oil, salt, and pepper. This dish is mostly prepared on the stove, mixed with cheese, and baked until it's gooey on the inside and crusty on top. This recipe will serve four to five, but I often make about a fourth of it for myself. It's super healthy (minus the Parmesan) and more delicious than it sounds, as long as you use enough salt and pepper when preparing the kale.

SERVES 4 TO 5

1 pound Barilla Plus or other whole wheat elbow pasta

2 to 3 cloves garlic, coarsely chopped

1 large white onion, chopped

4 tablespoons olive oil

1 bunch fresh kale, stems removed, torn into 1 to 2-inch pieces

1 to 2 cups water

Sea salt to taste

Freshly ground pepper to taste

1 teaspoon crushed red pepper, optional

2$\frac{1}{2}$ cups grated Parmesan cheese

Preheat oven to 350°F.

In a large pot, boil pasta according to package directions. Drain and set aside. In the same large pot over medium heat, sauté the garlic and onions in a few tablespoons of the olive oil. When the onions begin to brown around the edges, add the kale and stir. After a few minutes, the kale will turn a deep green. Pour $\frac{1}{2}$ cup of water over the kale (careful not to burn yourself with the splash!), add salt and pepper, and stir. Let the kale cook a little longer and repeat, adding $\frac{1}{4}$ cup of water at a time until the kale is cooked through and wilted. Continue to add a few pinches of salt and pepper to taste. Add the cooked pasta and 2 tablespoons of olive oil and stir. If you're going to add the crushed red pepper, add it now.

When the pasta and kale are mixed, add all but $\frac{1}{2}$ cup of the Parmesan. Stir and transfer to a buttered 2-quart baking dish.

Bake approximately 20 minutes, remove from the oven, and top with the remaining Parmesan cheese. Bake about 10 more minutes.

Tomato-Basil Polenta

FILE UNDER: **Not So Bad for You, Vegetarian (if you use vegetable broth)**

Polenta is a dish made from boiled cornmeal. A staple in Northern Italy, polenta has gone from being a peasant food to a rather high-priced item, especially when purchased in specialty stores. This polenta with a tomato-basil sauce on top is simple, light, and fresh—and you can make it with basic cornmeal. SERVES 4

1 (14 ounce) can chicken or vegetable broth

1 cup water

1 cup yellow cornmeal

2 tablespoons grated Parmesan cheese

Salt to taste

Freshly ground black pepper to taste

1/2 large white onion, chopped

2 cloves garlic, minced or pressed

2/3 tablespoon olive oil

1 (10 ounce) can crushed tomatoes

1/4 cup fresh basil, chopped

1/2 teaspoon crushed red pepper, optional

1/2 cup fresh mozzarella cheese, shredded

Preheat oven to 350°F.

In a medium saucepan over medium heat, combine and whisk together the broth, water, and cornmeal. When the mixture begins to boil, reduce heat to medium and stir. Add the Parmesan cheese while continuing to stir. Add salt and pepper to taste. Continue to stir for 7 to 8 minutes or until the mixture becomes very thick.

Transfer to a buttered or greased 8- or 9-inch square casserole dish. Set aside.

In the same saucepan over medium heat, sauté the onion and garlic in the olive oil. When the onions are translucent, add the crushed tomatoes and more salt and pepper to taste. When tomatoes are hot, add the chopped basil and crushed red pepper, if using.

Pour the tomato-basil sauce over the polenta, top with the mozzarella cheese, and bake, uncovered, for 15 to 20 minutes until the sauce and polenta are heated through and the cheese is melted.

Let stand 5 minutes before serving. Garnish with fresh basil.

Spuds au Gratin

FILE UNDER: Oh So Good but Bad for You, Vegetarian
(can be made gluten-free if you use a gluten-free cream of chicken soup)

You really can't go wrong with cheese and potatoes, no matter how you mix it. That's probably why some form of potatoes au gratin always places at my Annual Casserole Party. This recipe, courtesy of Diane Sylvester and Marie Argeris, placed second at the Second Annual Casserole Party. The recipe calls for Kefalograviera, a Greek cheese I can neither find nor pronounce. Feel free to substitute with Parmesan.

SERVES 6

1 stick butter

1 cup olive oil

3 to 4 cloves garlic, minced

2 large onions, sliced in rings

Salt to taste

1 tablespoon pepper

5 medium potatoes, peeled and thinly sliced

1 (16-ounce) carton sour cream

1 (12 to 14 ounce) can cream of chicken soup

1 pound cheddar cheese, shredded

$1/2$ cup Kefalograviera or Parmesan cheese, grated

1 teaspoon cayenne pepper

1 teaspoon paprika

Preheat oven to 375°F.

In a large frying pan, heat 2 to 3 tablespoons of the butter and a large drizzle of the olive oil and sauté half of the garlic with all of the onions. Once the onions are translucent and before they begin to brown, add the salt, pepper, and potato slices. (Because of the large amount of potatoes, you'll probably need to cook them in batches.) Make sure you always have enough butter and olive oil in the pan to keep the potatoes from sticking, and add salt and pepper to each batch. When each batch of potatoes is cooked, transfer to a buttered $9 1/2 \times 13$-inch baking dish.

In a separate bowl, mix the sour cream, remaining garlic, cream of chicken soup, and half of each of the cheeses, if using both. Add enough black pepper that you can see it (at least $1/2$ teaspoon) and about a teaspoon of cayenne pepper. Do not add salt at this point; there's enough in the soup. Pour mixture over the potatoes. Top with the remaining cheese and sprinkle with black pepper and the paprika.

Bake, uncovered, for 1 hour or until quite bubbly.

Let stand for 10 to 15 minutes before serving.

Classic Yellow Squash and Cracker Casserole

FILE UNDER: Oh So Good but Bad for You, Vegetarian

The epitome of a classic, monochromatic casserole, this yellow squash and cracker dish is made on the cheap and incorporates quite a few buttery crackers. Brighten it up with fresh chopped parsley or serve it with a mixed salad. If you don't mind the spice, add about a half teaspoon of cayenne pepper to highlight the flavor of the cheddar cheese. SERVES 6 TO 7

2 tablespoons butter

1 large white onion, diced

4 cups sliced yellow squash

Salt and pepper to taste

30 buttery round crackers, crushed

1½ cups cheddar cheese, shredded

2 eggs, beaten

½ cup milk

½ teaspoon brown sugar

2 tablespoons butter, melted

Olive oil as needed

½ teaspoon cayenne pepper, optional

Preheat oven to 400°F.

In a large skillet over medium heat, melt the 2 tablespoons of butter and sauté the onion until translucent. Add the squash and cook, stirring frequently, until tender, 5 to 10 minutes. If your squash is sticking, you can add a little olive oil or water to the pan. Sprinkle with salt and pepper. Remove from heat.

In a medium bowl, mix the cracker crumbs and cheese. Add half of the mixture to the squash and onions and mix well. Salt and pepper to taste (this is very important!). Transfer to a buttered 9×9-inch casserole dish.

In a small bowl, mix the eggs, milk, brown sugar, a few pinches of salt, and cayenne, if using. Pour over the casserole.

Mix the melted butter with the remaining cracker and cheese mixture and distribute evenly over the top of the casserole.

Bake, uncovered, 25 to 30 minutes or until golden brown on top.

Katy Sparks's Cauliflower Gratin

FILE UNDER: Oh So Good but Bad for You

This cauliflower gratin with goat cheese, cumin, and coriander is one of chef and cookbook author Katy Sparks's favorite dishes. As a side, it pairs well with lamb, duck, or chicken or is a great light lunch or brunch dish when served with salad and crusty bread. Katy suggests using leftovers as a base for poached eggs with a little smoked salmon. This can be served at room temperature with a drizzle of extra-virgin olive oil and a sprinkle of coarse sea salt to "wake up the flavors."

SERVES 6

1 clove garlic, slightly crushed

1 tablespoon unsalted butter

1 head of cauliflower, cut into florets

1 cup heavy cream

1/2 cup shredded Gruyère cheese

Freshly grated nutmeg to taste

Sea salt and pepper to taste

Cilantro for garnish, optional

Cheese Topping

1 (6 to 8 ounce) log fresh goat cheese

1 tablespoon extra-virgin olive oil

1/2 teaspoon whole cumin seeds, lightly toasted

1/2 teaspoon whole coriander seeds, lightly toasted

1 dried red chile (de arbol, peperoncini, Thai bird), crushed

1/2 teaspoon fresh thyme leaves

Zest of 1/2 lemon

Prepare the cheese topping by crumbling the goat cheese and gently folding in the olive oil, cumin, coriander, red chili, thyme, and lemon zest. Let stand at room temperature for 1 hour.

Preheat oven to 400°F.

Prepare a shallow-sided gratin dish that will accommodate all of the cauliflower in a thin, even layer by rubbing the bottom and sides with the garlic clove, then with the butter.

Cook the cauliflower florets in boiling salted water for 2 minutes until just tender. Drain and cool. Combine the cauliflower with the heavy cream and Gruyère and season to taste with the nutmeg, salt, and pepper.

Pour the cauliflower mixture into the prepared gratin dish.

Evenly dot the surface of the cauliflower with the marinated goat cheese. Place in the hot oven and cook until the sauce bubbles and the cheese has browned a little around the edges.

Serve hot or at room temperature garnished with fresh cilantro if desired.

Broccoli, Cheese, and Rice Casserole

FILE UNDER: Not So Bad for You, Gluten-Free, Vegetarian

A classic Midwestern dish, the Broccoli, Cheese, and Rice Casserole is a great way to get kids to eat their broccoli. In fact, it was the only way I'd eat it as a kid, even though the broccoli was from the freezer section, the rice was instant, and the cheese wasn't cheese at all (Velveeta, anyone?). In my first efforts to create a more perfect broccoli, cheese, and rice casserole, I failed miserably. Trying to make it easy on everyone, including myself, I thought I could get away with no stove-top preparation. I threw everything into a casserole dish uncooked, poured some creamy portobello mushroom soup on it, and more than an hour later, when I pulled a mess of hard yet soggy broccoli and crunchy rice with hot cream out of the oven, I almost understood the reason behind the Velveeta, instant rice, and frozen broccoli. So, there's some stove-top preparation involved in this one. Deal with it or hit the freezer section.

SERVES 5 TO 6

1 head of broccoli (about 2½ cups), chopped

1 large white onion, chopped

2 gloves garlic, minced or pressed

2 to 3 tablespoons olive oil

1 cup baby portobello mushrooms, cleaned and finely chopped

3 tablespoons butter

3 tablespoons flour

2 cups milk or half-and-half

Salt and pepper to taste

3 cups shredded cheddar cheese

1½ cups cooked long-grain rice

Preheat oven to 350°F.

Bring a medium pot of water with 1 teaspoon of salt to a boil. Add the chopped broccoli and cook, covered, for 3 to 4 minutes. Drain and set aside.

In the same pot over medium heat, sauté the onion and garlic in the olive oil, adding more olive oil as needed, until the onion is translucent. Add the mushrooms and sauté for about 1 minute, then add the butter. When the butter melts, add the flour and mix quickly and thoroughly. When the butter and flour are fully integrated, slowly add the milk, stirring constantly. Salt and pepper to taste, reduce the heat to low, and let simmer for 3 to 4 minutes, stirring occasionally.

When the milk mixture is hot, but not boiling, slowly add all but ½ cup of the cheddar cheese, stirring constantly. When the cheese begins to melt, add the rice and stir until everything is thoroughly mixed. Add the broccoli, salt and pepper to taste, remove from heat, and transfer to a 2½-quart baking dish and bake 20 to 25 minutes or until bubbly.

Remove from the oven and top with remaining cheese. Bake 5 to 10 more minutes or until cheese is melted and golden on top.

Let stand 10 minutes before serving.

Cauliflower and Poblano Gratin

FILE UNDER: Oh So Good but Bad for You, Gluten-Free, Vegetarian

A spicy take on a cauliflower and potato gratin, this recipe is courtesy of chefs Lizzy Singh Brar and Camille Becerra. Camille was a contestant on season three of Bravo's *Top Chef* and is owner and head chef of my favorite neighborhood restaurant, Paloma. This dish has more structure than most gratin dishes, which are often thrown together then put into the oven until they're done. For variation, you can leave out the cheese, though the dish won't be as rich, or substitute some of the cheddar cheese with pepper jack. SERVES 4 TO 5

3 poblano peppers

1 quart heavy cream

2 cloves garlic, whole

Salt and pepper

1 cup cave-aged cheddar cheese, grated

1 large head of cauliflower, thinly sliced or finely chopped

5 potatoes, thinly sliced (on a mandolin, if possible)

1 onion, thinly sliced

Preheat oven to 425°F.

Char whole poblanos on a gas burner. Transfer to a bowl, then cover with plastic wrap until they cool (this makes the peppers easier to peel and steams the insides). Peel the skins, remove the seeds, and roughly chop.

In a saucepan over medium heat, combine the chopped peppers, cream, and garlic. Season with a dash of salt and pepper, reduce the heat to low, and simmer for about 15 minutes, stirring occasionally. Remove the sauce from the heat and puree in a blender or food processor.

In a large mixing bowl, combine half of the poblano cream sauce, half of the cheese, and all of the cauliflower to make the poblano cauliflower sauce. Mix and salt and pepper to taste, if necessary.

In the bottom of a 2½-quart buttered baking dish, "shingle" or lay out the potato and onion slices like shingles, using enough to cover the bottom of the dish. Cover with half of the cauliflower mixture. Then neatly shingle another layer of the potato and onion (reserving some for one final layer). Cover with the remaining poblano cauliflower sauce and another layer of potato and onion. Cover with a lid or foil and bake for 1 hour.

Remove from oven and reduce the heat to 400°F. Top with the remaining cheese. When the oven has cooled, return the casserole to the oven, uncovered, and bake for an additional 15 minutes or until bubbly and golden brown on top.

Let stand 10 minutes before serving.

Zucchini and Sweet Corn Bake

FILE UNDER: **Not So Bad for You, Gluten-Free, Vegetarian**

I'm probably one of the few crazies who bake casseroles in the summertime. Luckily I have some friends who indulge me in my craziness. One of them always stops by the Greenmarket on her way to my apartment. And we have a system. She gets there, calls me to tell me what's available, and I try to make up the bare bones of a recipe on the spot.

One late summer afternoon she called and said there was an abundance of sweet corn on the cob and zucchini. I live off zucchini in the summer, so I told her to pick up a bunch of both. When she arrived, we decided to slice the zucchini, shuck the corn, and pour a little sauce over it. The result was an amazingly fresh, savory—yet sweet from the corn—simple summer casserole.

SERVES 4 TO 5

4 medium zucchini, thinly sliced

Corn from 2 cobs of fresh corn

1 large white onion, finely chopped

3 cloves garlic, minced

1 cup Parmesan cheese

8 ounces sour cream

$1/4$ teaspoon black pepper

1 teaspoon sea salt

2 eggs

Preheat oven to 400°F.

In a 2 to $2^{1}/_{2}$-quart casserole dish, mix the zucchini and corn.

In a mixing bowl, combine the remaining ingredients. Pour the mixture over the casserole, cover, and bake 35 to 40 minutes. Remove the cover, stir, and bake an additional 10 to 15 minutes.

Let stand 10 minutes before serving.

Thanksgiving Kugel

FILE UNDER: Oh So Good but Bad for You, Vegetarian

Kugel (Yiddish: n. kugl or koogel or kigel, as was pronounced in Galicia/Central Europe) is any one of a wide variety of traditional baked Jewish side dishes or desserts, and can be sweet or savory. It is sometimes translated as "pudding" or "casserole."

This Thanksgiving Kugel took home the best non-savory title at my Third Annual Casserole Party, though it was created by two Gentiles, Lacey Tauber and Bryan Tooze. SERVES 4 TO 5

3/4 pound egg noodles

1 (8 ounce) carton small-curd cottage cheese

1 (8 ounce) carton sour cream

1/2 cup milk

1/8 cup sugar

1 stick butter, melted

Pinch of salt

1 tablespoon cinnamon

1 1/2 cups pumpkin pie filling

Raisins and dried cranberries (about 1/4 cup each)

3 eggs, beaten

Topping

1 stick cold butter

1/2 cup flour

1/2 cup brown sugar

1 teaspoon nutmeg

Preheat oven to 375°F.

In a large pot, boil the egg noodles to just under al dente. Drain and set aside.

In a large mixing bowl, combine the cottage cheese, sour cream, milk, sugar, melted butter, salt, cinnamon, pumpkin pie filling, raisins, and cranberries. Add the noodles and mix until all of the noodles are coated. Pour the mixture into a greased 2 1/2 to 3-quart casserole dish. Pour the eggs over the top of the casserole.

For the topping, carefully mix the cold butter with flour, brown sugar, and nutmeg to create a crumbly mixture. Pour crumbles over the top of the casserole after the egg.

Bake, covered, for half an hour and uncovered for another half hour.

Can be served hot or cold.

Bacon and Potato Yummy Stuff

FILE UNDER: Not So Bad for You, Gluten-Free, Vegetarian

My friend la Fourmyle has celiac disease, meaning she's allergic to wheat gluten. While she doesn't get to partake in the joys of regular pasta and bread, she still manages to come up with the most decadent and starchy meals, and this potato and onion "yummy stuff" is no exception. Did I mention it's super, super simple? Just make sure you use enough salt and pepper to keep it really flavorful.   SERVES 4 TO 6

2 tablespoons butter

2 tablespoons gluten-free or rice flour

2 cups milk

Salt and pepper

4 to 5 large baking potatoes, peeled and thinly sliced

2 large white onions, chopped

1 pound bacon, cut into 1-inch pieces

Preheat oven to 375°F.

In a small saucepan over medium heat, melt the butter. Add the flour and stir until the butter and flour are well combined. Reduce heat to low and slowly pour in the milk, stirring constantly until it thickens (3 to 5 minutes). Add salt and a dash of pepper to taste. Set aside.

Cover the bottom of a buttered 2½-quart baking dish with a layer of the potatoes. Sprinkle a good portion of the onion (a handful or two) on top of the potatoes, and then add a layer of the bacon. Salt and pepper generously. Continue layering, finishing with potatoes on top. Pour the white sauce over the dish, making sure every potato on top is covered.

Bake, covered, for approximately 1 hour or until the sauce is bubbling at the bottom. Remove cover and bake for an additional 15 to 20 minutes or until the top layer of potatoes reaches that lovely, crispy brown!

Let stand for 10 minutes before serving.

Cheesy Rice with Chiles

FILE UNDER: Oh So Good but Bad for You, Gluten-Free, Vegetarian

A sometimes-bland rice dish is given a kick with extra-sharp cheddar—which is enhanced by cayenne pepper. This spicy dish goes really well with chicken and is best served warm, so the cheese is nice and gooey. Substitute fresh jalapeños or habañeros for the canned chiles if you're so inclined.   SERVES 4

1 large white onion, finely chopped	1 can green chiles, drained and minced
4 tablespoons butter	1 tablespoon chopped fresh parsley
4 cups cooked white rice	2 cups grated extra-sharp cheddar
2 cups sour cream	$1/2$ teaspoon cayenne pepper
1 cup cream-style cottage cheese	Salt and pepper to taste

Preheat oven to 350°F.

In a large skillet over medium heat, sauté the onion in the butter until the onions begin to brown around the edges. Remove the skillet from heat and mix in the rice, sour cream, cottage cheese, chiles, parsley, $1^{1}/_{2}$ cups of the cheddar cheese, the cayenne pepper, salt, and pepper.

Transfer the rice mixture to a buttered or greased $2^{1}/_{2}$-quart baking dish. Cover with remaining cheddar cheese and bake, uncovered, for 25 to 30 minutes or until bubbly.

Beet and Potato au Gratin

FILE UNDER: Oh So Good but Bad for You

I grew up on canned beets, which turned me off them for much of my adult life. When I finally tried a roasted fresh beet, at the behest of an old boyfriend, I became obsessed with boiled and roasted beets. I still won't eat them pickled, but I will most certainly bake them with potatoes and Gorgonzola cheese. This dish is very rich, and turns pink during the baking process. Don't be alarmed by the color.

SERVES 4 TO 6

5 baking potatoes, peeled and thinly sliced

5 medium to large beets, peeled and thinly sliced

2 cups heavy cream

3 tablespoons butter, melted

$1/2$ teaspoon freshly grated pepper

10 ounces Gorgonzola cheese, crumbled

2 tablespoons fresh chopped parsley

Preheat oven to 400°F.

Layer the potatoes and beets in a 2¾-quart greased or buttered baking dish.

In a mixing bowl, combine the heavy cream, melted butter, pepper, all but one ounce of the Gorgonzola cheese, and half of the chopped parsley. Stir until everything is well integrated. Pour over the potatoes and beets and toss a few times.

Bake, covered, for 1 hour or until the potatoes and beets are cooked through. Remove cover and sprinkle the remaining cheese and parsley on top. Finish with a dash of freshly grated pepper, and bake an additional 10 minutes.

Let stand 5 to 10 minutes before serving.

Beets with Potato and Bacon

This gratin with a kick has bacon *and* a crusty bacon-infused bread crumb topping. The bacon adds a savory touch to the rich dish, and the potatoes maintain a subtle base to counteract the richness of the beets, Gorgonzola, and bacon. While this requires a little more stove-top preparation than a conventional gratin, the crusty topping and crispy bacon are well worth it.

SERVES 4 TO 6

1/2 pound bacon

5 baking potatoes, peeled and thinly sliced

5 medium to large beets, peeled and thinly sliced

2 cups heavy cream

3 tablespoons butter, melted

1/2 teaspoon freshly grated pepper

10 ounces Gorgonzola cheese, crumbled

2 tablespoons fresh chopped parsley

1/2 cup dried bread crumbs

Preheat oven to 400°F.

In a skillet or pan over medium heat, cook the bacon until it is almost crispy. Remove the bacon from the pan, reserving the bacon grease. Let the bacon cool.

Layer the potatoes and beets in a 2³/₄-quart greased or buttered baking dish.

Finely chop the cooled bacon.

In a mixing bowl, stir together the heavy cream, melted butter, pepper, Gorgonzola, and half of the chopped parsley until everything is well integrated. Add all but 1/4 cup of the bacon, mix well, and pour over the beets and potatoes, tossing a few times.

Bake, covered, for 1 hour or until potatoes and beets are cooked through.

While the casserole is baking, sauté the bread crumbs and remaining parsley in the bacon grease for 1 to 2 minutes.

Remove the cover from the casserole, sprinkle the bread crumb mixture and remaining bacon on top, and bake an additional 10 minutes.

Let stand 5 to 10 minutes before serving.

Classic Green Bean Casserole

FILE UNDER: **Not So Bad for You, Vegetarian**

I grew up on green bean casserole. Upon moving to Brooklyn and making my own, however, I realized this was not at all my mom's green bean casserole but the recipe from every brand of French fried onion can, cream of mushroom soup can, and cookbook in the world. I still love it and would be remiss not to include it, even though I've made a few changes to make it my own.

SERVES 6

1 (10.75 ounce) can condensed cream of mushroom soup

$\frac{1}{2}$ cup milk

Salt and pepper to taste

$\frac{1}{2}$ large white onion, chopped

$\frac{1}{2}$ cup cleaned and chopped baby portobello mushrooms

4 cups cooked green beans

$1\frac{1}{3}$ cups French fried onions

Preheat oven to 350°F.

Mix the soup, milk, salt, pepper, onions, and mushrooms in a 2-quart casserole dish. Stir in the beans and $\frac{2}{3}$ cup of the fried onions. Bake for about 25 minutes. Top with the remaining $\frac{2}{3}$ cup of fried onions and bake about 5 more minutes, until onions are lightly browned.

Sweet Sausage with Sweet Peppers

This dish travels well because it's nearly as good cold as it is hot. But if you're going to serve it cold, make it look like you meant to by sprinkling some fresh chopped parsley or cilantro on top. The Parmesan can be substituted with feta, or this dish can easily be made lactose-free by eliminating the cheese. If you're not used to cooking with sausage, remember to remove the casing before you cook it (a lesson I learned the hard way).   SERVES 6

1 large white onion, chopped	1 teaspoon crushed red pepper
2 to 3 tablespoons olive oil	1/2 teaspoon salt
1 pound sweet sausage, casing removed	1/2 teaspoon pepper
1 pound orzo	2 large sweet yellow peppers, chopped
2 cups white wine	1/2 cup Parmesan cheese, grated
2 cups chicken or vegetable stock	

Preheat oven to 400°F.

In a large skillet over medium heat, sauté the onion in the olive oil until translucent. Add the sausage to the skillet and crumble with a wooden spoon. When the sausage is browned, remove from heat and set aside.

In a 2³/₄-quart baking dish, mix together the orzo, white wine, stock, red pepper, salt, and pepper. Add the sausage and onions, peppers, and Parmesan and mix well.

Bake, covered, for about an hour. For best results, stir once or twice while baking. Remove cover and bake an additional 5 to 10 minutes.

Let stand 5 to 10 minutes before serving or serve cold with fresh chopped cilantro or parsley.

Cheesy Green Beans and Bacon

Here's a take on another classic dish. Bacon is a great way to spruce up green beans. If I recall, I think you can actually buy a can of green beans and bacon. Don't do that. Ever. This is a much, much better alternative and uses fresh, whole ingredients.　　SERVES 5 TO 6

2 pounds fresh green beans, ends removed and snapped in half

$1/2$ pound thick-cut bacon

2 tablespoons flour

1 cup milk

$1/2$ cup chopped baby portobello mushrooms

$1/2$ teaspoon nutmeg

$1/4$ teaspoon freshly ground pepper

Salt to taste

1 cup shredded cheddar cheese

Preheat oven to 350°F.

Cook the green beans in a pot of boiling salted water for 2 to 3 minutes. Drain, rinse with cold water, and set aside.

In the same pot over medium heat, cook the bacon but don't let it get crispy. Remove the bacon, reserving the grease.

Add the flour to the bacon grease, stirring quickly. Add the milk, mushrooms, nutmeg, pepper, and salt. When the mixture is hot, add the cheese and reduce heat to low. When the cheese is melted, add the green beans and mix well.

Transfer to a lightly greased 2-quart casserole dish and top with crumbled bacon. Bake, uncovered, about 30 minutes or until bubbly.

Simple Lentil Bake

FILE UNDER: **Not So Bad for You, Vegetarian**

High in protein and flavor, this lentil bake is colorful and makes a great side dish. Lentils are flavorful little legumes that are sometimes overlooked in baking. They're often used in soup or to top something off, but mixed with cheese, mushrooms, and onions, they can be the star of a one-dish meal. This dish requires you to spend some time standing over the stove, but if you use mixed lentils, at least you'll have something pretty to look at.   SERVES 4 TO 6

2$\frac{1}{2}$ cups mixed lentils (brown, green, and/or red), dry

1 large white onion, finely chopped

6 cloves garlic, minced or pressed

4 tablespoons olive oil

2 cups chopped baby portobello mushrooms

2 cups vegetable broth

2 tablespoons flour

16 ounces pureed tomatoes

2$\frac{1}{4}$ cups Parmesan cheese

Salt and pepper

Preheat oven to 350°F.

Place the lentils and enough water to come 1$\frac{1}{2}$ inches over them in a medium saucepan. Bring to a boil over high heat. When the water is boiling, reduce heat to low and simmer, covered, until lentils are barely tender. Drain and set aside.

In the bottom of the same saucepan over medium heat, sauté the onion and garlic in the olive oil until the onions are translucent. Add the mushrooms and sauté 1 to 2 minutes. Add the vegetable broth and flour. Mix well and add the tomatoes. Set heat to high and bring sauce to a boil. When the sauce is boiling, reduce heat to low and stir in the lentils. When the lentils are coated, add 2 cups of the Parmesan cheese, salt, and pepper. Mix well and transfer to a greased 2$\frac{1}{2}$-quart casserole dish. Cover with the remaining cheese and bake, uncovered, 30 to 35 minutes.

Zucc & Tom

FILE UNDER: Not So Bad for You, Gluten-Free, Vegetarian

This easy zucchini and tomato casserole, courtesy of my old friend Berkeley Bob, requires no stove-top preparation and cooks really quickly. The trick is to not let it get too soupy, so eye the mix depending on how much zucchini you use. And if you use a little too much tomato juice, then your casserole will be a little soupy. And that's the worst that can happen.

SERVES 4

2 to 3 large zucchini, cut into ¼-inch slices

1 large yellow onion, finely chopped

1 (28 ounce) can crushed tomatoes, drained, juice reserved

¼ teaspoon salt

¼ teaspoon pepper

¼ pound sharp white cheddar, shredded

¼ pound cheddar, shredded

1 tablespoon fresh chopped basil

Preheat oven to 350°F.

Toss the zucchini, onion, and ¼ cup of the tomato juice with salt and pepper in a shallow casserole dish. Bake, uncovered, 10 to 15 minutes.

Remove from the oven and toss ¾ of the cheese and the crushed tomatoes with the zucchini and onion. Sprinkle with the basil and more pepper to taste. Top with the remainder of the cheese.

Turn oven down to 300°F and bake for 15 to 20 more minutes.

Potato and Kale Bake

FILE UNDER: Not So Bad for You, Gluten-Free, Vegetarian

Mashed potatoes baked with sautéed kale, this creamy, savory side is a great way to sneak some nutrients into a meal. Kale is one of the most flavorful and vitamin packed of the green leafy vegetables and goes so well with potatoes. This goes great with a cut of red meat and a glass of red wine. I leave the skins on my potatoes, but feel free to peel them.

SERVES 5 TO 6

2 pounds baking potatoes, cubed

1 large white onion, chopped

4 cloves garlic, sliced

3 tablespoons olive oil

1 large bunch kale, stems removed

1 cup sour cream

4 tablespoons butter, melted

Salt and pepper to taste

Preheat oven to 375°F.

In a large pot over medium heat, boil the potatoes for 10 to 20 minutes or until you can easily stick a fork through them and pull it out. Drain, mash, and set aside.

In the bottom of the same large pot over medium heat, sauté the onion and garlic in the olive oil until the onions are translucent. Begin to add the kale, quickly tearing it into bite-size pieces and adding it to the pot. When all of the kale is in the pot, mix well and add a dash of salt and pepper. Sauté the kale for about 10 minutes, adding ¼ cup water to the pot at least once while cooking.

While the kale is cooking, in a large mixing bowl mash the potatoes with the sour cream and melted butter, and salt and pepper to taste. Mix well, then add the kale, onions, and garlic. Mix well and transfer to a lightly greased 2½-quart casserole dish. Bake, uncovered, 35 to 40 minutes or until golden brown on top.

Let stand 5 minutes before serving.

Savory Spinach and Artichoke Casserole

FILE UNDER: Oh So Good but Bad for You, Gluten-Free, Vegetarian

Similar to a spinach-artichoke dip, but with more spinach and artichoke and less dip (cream cheese), this is a tad healthier, at least bite per bite. It's chockfull of spinach, and goes well with red or white meat and red or white wine. Be sure to drain as much of the water from the spinach as you can, or you'll end up with a runny casserole. SERVES 6 TO 8

2 (8 ounce) packages cream cheese, softened

1/2 cup milk

4 (10 ounce) packages frozen chopped spinach, thawed and drained

1 1/2 cups grated Parmesan cheese

1 (10.75 ounce) can artichoke hearts, drained and chopped

Salt and pepper

Preheat oven to 350°F.

In a large mixing bowl, combine the cream cheese and milk and mix until blended. Gradually add the spinach, mixing well. Add the Parmesan and artichoke hearts and mix well. Salt and pepper to taste. Transfer mixture to a 2 to 2 1/2-quart casserole dish.

Bake, uncovered, for 35 to 40 minutes.

Those who didn't grow up on casseroles or haven't cooked regularly for multiple dinner guests might not appreciate the beauty of the one-dish dinner. While it's often an inexpensive way to feed a family, it's also an easy way to entertain. Some of the main-dish casseroles in this book can be made for ten to fifteen dollars. For others you'll spend upward of seventy-five dollars on ingredients.

But one casserole generally feeds five to six people, ten to twelve if it's on the larger side. If you're making a casserole for yourself, you can live off it for days, and most casseroles only get better the more they're reheated in the oven—and they're not so bad in the microwave, either.

Because I'm rarely one to let food go to waste, many of these casseroles incorporate leftover ingredients, like my Thanksgiving Casserole, which obviously calls for leftover turkey, and Chef Ron Silver's Tweed Kettle Pie, which is a great way to use leftover salmon.

Whether you use fresh or leftover ingredients, or a combination of both, there are endless possibilities when it comes to casseroles, because you're simply baking things you like together in one dish.

The Greenpoint

I live in Greenpoint—a predominantly Polish neighborhood in northern Brooklyn—and I'm obsessed with the flavors here: kielbasa, cheese, mushroom, potato, and sauerkraut. I always said I wish I could mash all the flavors together so I could have them all at once, so one day, instead of making one giant pierogi, I made this casserole. The peas give the drab-looking dish much-needed color, and little green points, of course. I suggest a creamy portobello mushroom soup for this, but any old cream of mushroom soup will do. SERVES 6 TO 7

1 pound rotelle (wheel-shaped) pasta

1 large heat-and-serve kielbasa

1 large white onion, finely chopped

2 cups sauerkraut

4 tablespoons olive oil

2 large portobello mushrooms, finely chopped

2 cups creamy portobello or other mushroom soup

1 cup grated Parmesan cheese

Salt and pepper

16 ounces frozen sweet peas

Potato chips, optional

Preheat oven to 350°F.

Boil pasta in a large pot of salted water. Cook to just under al dente, drain, and set aside.

Cut the kielbasa into ¼-inch slices. In a large saucepan over high heat, sauté the kielbasa slices, onion, and sauerkraut in the olive oil. When the kielbasa is browned, add the mushrooms and sauté the mixture for another 3 to 5 minutes.

In a large pot over low heat, mix the kielbasa mixture and the soup. When well mixed, add the pasta. When the pasta is well coated with the soup, add ¾ cup of the Parmesan while continuing to stir. Salt and pepper to taste. Add the frozen peas (they can, and should, go in frozen) and stir.

Transfer mixture to a greased 2½-quart casserole dish. Sprinkle the remaining ¼ cup Parmesan on top of the casserole.

Bake, uncovered, 40 to 45 minutes or until slightly brown on top.

OPTIONAL: Once the casserole has browned, add a few handfuls of crushed potato chips (covered with a light sprinkling of Parmesan cheese) and bake for an additional 5 to 10 minutes or until chips become golden brown.

The Shameless Carnivore's Pigeon Potpie

FILE UNDER: Oh So Good but Bad for You

You might know Scott Gold from his book *The Shameless Carnivore: A Manifesto for Meat Lovers*. The memoir documents two years of Scott's traveling, hunting, butchering, cooking, and eating everything from caribou steaks to alligators, snails, and guinea pigs. It was with great excitement—coupled with slight trepidation on my part—that he and I decided on this pigeon potpie recipe for my book. "Squabs," said Scott, "which are actually either young, un-fledged (that is, "flightless" and thus very tender) pigeons or doves, are possessed of a power-fully dark, rich, and fragrant meat that lends this dish a unique quality you won't find in your standard cafeteria potpie, and one that will make you look like a bona fide gourmet when you make it, even if, like me, your culinary skills are somewhat questionable."

Where does one find pigeon other than the mean streets of New York? According to Scott, at any reputable butcher shop. If that's not the case where you live, or you just can't bring yourself to eat pigeon (which is surprisingly good, when prepared well), substitute with duck, but not chicken—that bird is too boring for this dish, claims the Shameless Carnivore.

VARIATION: If you're going to the trouble of acquiring squab, you might be one to make your own piecrust and biscuit mix. If so, the super-easy recipes are included below; if not, ready-made will do just fine.

SERVES 5 TO 6

1 ready-made 9-inch piecrust

2 (12 ounce) pigeons (squabs)

Salt and pepper to taste

2 cups biscuit mix

1/2 cup milk

6 tablespoons butter

6 tablespoons white flour

1 1/2 cups chicken broth

1/2 teaspoon Worcestershire sauce

2 dashes freshly ground black pepper

1/2 teaspoon thyme

1/2 teaspoon rosemary

1/2 cup white onion, minced

1 1/2 cups frozen peas and carrots, cooked and drained

Prepare piecrust according to package directions.

Preheat oven to 350°F.

Clean and pat dry the two squabs, then lightly dust in salt and pepper. Place the birds breast-side-up on a lightly greased baking dish and bake for 30 to 45 minutes, until meat is just barely done (squab and duck taste best slightly on the rare side). Remove from dish and let stand until cool enough to pick all the meat from the bones. Reserve meat.

Set oven temperature to 425°F.

Combine biscuit mix and milk, and knead thoroughly until dough is about 1/2-inch thick.

In a medium saucepan over medium heat, melt the butter. Add the flour and stir continuously. When the roux is smooth and beginning to bubble, add the chicken broth, Worcestershire sauce, pepper, thyme, and rosemary. Simmer and stir continuously until thick.

Place pigeon meat, onions, peas, and carrots in piecrust, and pour filling to cover. Top crust with biscuit dough, and brush the top lightly with milk. Cook until done, approximately 30 minutes. Let stand for 5 to 10 minutes before serving.

Piecrust

1 cup flour	6 tablespoons cold unsalted butter, cubed
1/2 teaspoon salt	1 to 3 teaspoons cold water

Combine the flour and salt in a bowl. Cut in the butter using a pastry cutter or your fingers until the butter pieces are no larger than a pea. Add the cold water one teaspoon at a time, mixing the dough with your hands until it just comes together and forms a ball. Roll out onto waxed paper or parchment paper, and press into the bottom of a pie pan. This does not need to be prebaked.

Biscuit Mix

1 1/2 cups flour	1/2 teaspoon salt
2 teaspoons baking powder	1 stick butter
2 teaspoons sugar	1/2 cup milk

Combine the flour, baking powder, sugar, and salt in a bowl. Cut in the butter with a pastry cutter or your fingers until the mixture resembles coarse crumbs. Add the milk and stir with a fork or wooden spoon until the dough is fully moistened. Turn onto a floured surface and roll or press out to a round, thick wheel roughly the size of the top of the pie.

When the pie filling has been made, simply pour it into the prepared pan with the bottom crust in it. Top the filling mixture with the biscuit top, loosely cinch the edges shut with your fingers, and bake.

Beef and Spinach Pie

Slightly spicy beef with spinach and cheese, baked in a piecrust? If I still cared about the four food groups, I'd be really excited that this covers all of them. A delicious and savory pie, this goes really well with red wine. And there you have it: dinner. You can easily halve this recipe, because it actually makes two pies.

SERVES 10 TO 12

2 premade 9-inch frozen pastry or pie shells

1 large white onion, chopped

2 cloves garlic, minced or pressed

3 tablespoons olive oil

1/2 cup sliced baby portobello mushrooms

1 pound lean ground sirloin

1/4 teaspoon cayenne pepper

1/2 teaspoon chili powder

1 teaspoon oregano

Salt and pepper

16 ounces pureed tomatoes

2 tablespoon fresh chopped basil

1 (10 ounce) package frozen chopped spinach, thawed and drained

1 cup ricotta cheese

1 1/2 cups shredded mozzarella cheese

Preheat oven to 400°F.

Bake pie shells according to package directions. I use Pillsbury, and they cook for about 11 minutes. Remove the shells when they're golden brown, and reduce the oven temperature to 350°F.

In a large skillet over medium heat, sauté the onion and garlic in the olive oil until the onions are translucent. Add the mushrooms, beef, cayenne, chili powder, oregano, and salt and pepper to taste. When the beef is cooked through, add the tomatoes and 1 tablespoon of the basil. Set the heat to high and cook, stirring occasionally, until the sauce is boiling, then reduce heat to low. Let simmer 5 to 10 minutes.

In a medium bowl, mix the spinach, ricotta cheese, and 1/2 cup of the mozzarella. Spoon the spinach mixture evenly into the bottom of each cooled crust, then cover evenly with the meat sauce. Top with the remaining mozzarella and basil. Bake, uncovered, for 35 to 40 minutes or until the mozzarella begins to brown and the pie is hot throughout.

Let stand 5 to 10 minutes before serving.

Pearl's Pizza Casserole

FILE UNDER: Not So Bad for You

On Mondays I pick up a seven-year-old girl from school. We go to the grocery store then to her house to make a meal for the family's dinner (after her homework is done, of course). Often I have no idea what I'm going to make when I arrive at school, so I let her suggestions guide my menu. One afternoon she really wanted pizza, but we compromised and decided on a pizza casserole instead.

SERVES 5 TO 6

1 (12 ounce) package large egg noodles

2 to 3 tablespoons olive oil

1 large white onion, diced

5 cloves garlic, minced

1 large green bell pepper, diced

1 pound ground beef

1 to 3 teaspoons crushed red pepper to taste

Salt and pepper to taste

1 (28 ounce) can pureed tomatoes

2 tablespoons dried basil (or 4 tablespoons fresh and minced if available)

1½ tablespoons oregano

8 to 10 ounces shredded mozzarella

1½ cups baby portobello mushrooms, sliced

Preheat oven to 350°F.

In a large pot, parboil the egg noodles (add a little olive oil and salt to the water), but be sure to take them out just under al dente. Run cold water over the noodles to stop the cooking, drain, and set aside in the strainer.

In the same large pot, over medium heat, sauté the onion and garlic in the olive oil. When the onions begin to brown, reduce the heat to low, add the green peppers, and let them cook for about a minute. Add the beef, and when it begins to brown, add the crushed red pepper, salt, and pepper. Once the beef is well seasoned, add the tomatoes and mix well. When the meat is fully coated in the tomatoes, add the egg noodles while continuing to stir. Add the basil and oregano and more crushed red pepper as needed. Mix in half of the mozzarella, mix well, and then add the mushrooms (they should go in at the last minute).

Transfer to a 2³/₄-quart buttered or greased baking dish. Sprinkle half of the remaining mozzarella (about ¹/₄ cup) on top.

Bake, uncovered, 35 to 45 minutes.

Remove when bubbly and top with the remaining mozzarella. Bake an additional 10 minutes or until the cheese is melted and begins to brown.

Let stand for 10 minutes before serving.

Chicken or Turkey Tetrazzini

FILE UNDER: Oh So Good but Bad for You

This dish is supposedly named after the opera singer Luisa Tetrazzini who, let's just say, died fat and happy. In fact, she was known for saying, "I am old, I am fat, but I am still Tetrazzini." I'd like to imagine her in her muumuu eating lots of spaghetti and incorporating whatever meat leftovers she had around the house, because this dish is great for incorporating leftover chicken or turkey.   SERVES 4 (OR 2 VERY HUNGRY OPERA SINGERS)

1/2 pound spaghetti noodles, broken in half

1 large white onion, chopped

2 cloves garlic, minced or pressed

2 to 3 tablespoons olive oil

1 tablespoon dried basil

1 teaspoon dried oregano

1 cup heavy cream

2 tablespoons flour

1 cup chicken broth

1 cup baby portobello mushrooms, cleaned and chopped

Cayenne pepper to taste

1/4 tablespoon salt

1/4 tablespoon pepper

2 cups shredded cooked chicken or turkey

1 1/4 cups Parmesan cheese, grated

1 tablespoon butter, melted

1/4 cup bread crumbs

Preheat oven to 350°F.

In a large pot of boiling water, cook the spaghetti until just under al dente. Drain and set aside.

In the same large pot, over medium heat, sauté the onions and garlic in the olive oil until the onions are translucent. Add the basil and oregano. Mix well and add the cream and flour. Mix well and add the chicken broth. When the mixture begins to simmer, reduce the heat to low and add the mushrooms. Cook the mixture on low for 1 to 2 minutes, then add the cayenne, salt, pepper, and the chicken or turkey. Mix well and add 1 cup of the Parmesan. Add the pasta and mix until the noodles are fully coated. Add more salt and pepper to taste, if needed, then transfer to a lightly greased 2 to 2 1/2-quart casserole dish.

In a small bowl, mix the melted butter, remaining Parmesan, and bread crumbs. Put half of this mixture on top of the casserole, then bake, uncovered, for 30 minutes or until the casserole is bubbly and the top is golden brown. Remove, add the remaining topping, and bake for an additional 10 minutes.

Let stand 5 minutes before serving.

Throwdown Eggplant Parmesan

FILE UNDER: Oh So Good but Bad for You, Vegetarian

I'm a huge fan of Bobby Flay and his Food Network show *Throwdown*, on which he ambushes food experts and challenges them to their signature dishes, with the help of the Food Network kitchen staff. Sometimes he wins, sometimes not. This Eggplant Parmesan is from a recent challenge, and as far as I'm concerned, it's a winner. Not the simplest recipe in the world, it's broken into two parts, so pay close attention and enjoy.

SERVES: 6 TO 8

Roasted Red Pepper Tomato Sauce

3 tablespoons olive oil

1 large yellow onion, coarsely chopped

3 cloves garlic, coarsely chopped

1/2 teaspoon red pepper flakes

3 roasted red peppers, peeled, seeded, and chopped

2 (28 ounce) cans plum tomatoes and their juices, crushed with your hands

3 tablespoons chopped flat-leaf parsley

3 tablespoons chopped fresh basil

1 tablespoon chopped fresh oregano

Salt and freshly ground black pepper

Honey, optional

Heat the oil in a large Dutch oven over medium-high heat. Add the onion and cook until soft. Add the garlic and red pepper flakes and cook for 1 minute. Add the red peppers and cook for 1 minute.

Add the tomatoes, bring to a boil, and cook, stirring occasionally, until thickened, about 25 to 30 minutes. Transfer the mixture to a food processor and process until smooth. Return the mixture to the pot, add the parsley, basil, and oregano and season with salt and pepper. Cook for 10 minutes longer, and season with honey, if needed.

Eggplant

5 cups fresh dried bread crumbs (see Tip below)

3 tablespoons finely chopped fresh flat-leaf parsley

1 tablespoon finely chopped fresh oregano

1 tablespoon finely chopped fresh thyme

2 1/2 teaspoons salt

3/4 teaspoon freshly ground black pepper

2 cups all-purpose flour

6 large eggs, beaten

Vegetable oil for frying

2 to 3 medium eggplants (about 2 1/4 pounds), cut into 1/2-inch-thick round slices (about 18 slices)

12 ounces grated mozzarella (not fresh)

12 ounces grated Fontina

3/4 cup grated Pecorino Romano

Fresh basil leaves, torn

1/2 pound fresh mozzarella, thinly sliced

TIP: To dry out the bread crumbs: Preheat oven to 300°F. Evenly spread the bread crumbs on a large baking sheet and place in the oven. Bake for 5 minutes, turn the oven off and let the bread crumbs sit in the oven for 30 minutes or until just dry. For best results, use day-old bread.

Preheat the oven to 400°F.

Put the bread crumbs in a large shallow bowl, add the herbs, 1 1/2 teaspoons of the salt, and 1/2 teaspoon of the pepper, and mix until combined.

Place flour in a medium shallow bowl or on a large plate and season with 1 teaspoon of salt and 1/4 teaspoon of pepper. In another medium shallow bowl, whisk the eggs and 2 tablespoons of water together.

Season each eggplant slice on both sides with salt and pepper. Dredge each eggplant slice in the flour to coat, tapping off excess, then dip it in the egg, and finally dredge it in the bread crumb mixture. Shake off any excess breading and transfer the eggplant to a baking sheet. Repeat with the remaining eggplant.

Heat 1/2 inch of oil in 2 large straight-sided sauté pans over medium heat until the oil reaches a temperature of 385° F. Working in small batches, fry a few of the eggplant slices, turning once, until golden brown, about 3 minutes per batch. Using tongs, transfer to a paper towel–lined baking sheet. Repeat with the remaining eggplant.

Lightly butter a $15 \times 10 \times 2$-inch baking dish. Cover the bottom of the baking dish with some of the tomato sauce and arrange a third of the eggplant over the sauce. Cover the eggplant with some of the sauce, grated mozzarella, Fontina, Romano, and some of the basil. Repeat to make 3 layers, ending with the sauce. Top with the fresh mozzarella and remaining Romano and bake until hot and just beginning to brown, about 30 minutes. Let stand 10 minutes before serving.

King Ranch Chicken

This classic South Texas dish is loathed and admired in equal parts by Texans. Andrew Schmidt, who shared his mom's recipe, claims it's the reason he was a fat kid. "I had it once a week," he said. "At least." This casserole is made in two parts: the sauce and the layers. The chicken broth is key, as it keeps the dish from drying out. I added the option of cayenne pepper for some extra kick, although jalapeños are probably more Texan. Add tortilla chips or Doritos on top to annoy the naturalists. SERVES 6

1 whole chicken, boiled, boned, and cut or torn into bite-size pieces, broth reserved

1 dozen corn tortillas, cut or torn into bite-size pieces

2 cups grated cheddar cheese

2 large yellow onions, finely chopped

1 (10.5 ounce) can cream of chicken soup

1 (10.5 ounce) can cream of mushroom soup

1 (10 ounce) can Ro-tel or other tomatoes with chiles

1½ cups chicken broth (from boiled chicken)

½ to 1 teaspoon cayenne pepper

Salt and pepper

Tortilla chips or Doritos, optional

Preheat oven to 350°F.

Layer the chicken, tortillas, cheese, and onion in a greased 9×13-inch casserole dish.

In a blender or by hand, combine the cream of chicken soup, cream of mushroom soup, tomatoes, chicken broth, and cayenne. Salt and pepper to taste. Pour the sauce over the casserole.

Bake, uncovered, for 35 to 45 minutes or until bubbly.

OPTIONAL: Top with a few handfuls of crushed Doritos or tortilla chips after you remove the casserole from the oven.

Spicy Shrimp with Rice

FILE UNDER: **Not So Bad for You, Gluten-Free, Lactose-Free**

This super-simple spicy shrimp casserole is prepared on the stove top and transferred to a casserole dish for baking. The rice will cook in the oven, as long as you remember to cover it before it goes in. You can use fresh or frozen shrimp, but if using frozen, thaw before using. Also remember to remove the tails from the shrimp. There's nothing worse than diving into a one-dish dinner and finding something that doesn't belong.   SERVES 4 TO 5

2 cloves garlic, minced	12 ounces pureed tomatoes
1 large white onion, chopped	$1/2$ teaspoon cayenne pepper
3 to 4 teaspoons olive oil	Pinch of chili powder, to taste
$1^{1}/_{2}$ cups chicken stock	Salt and pepper
1 cup uncooked white rice	$1/2$ pound small shrimp, deveined

Preheat oven to 375°F.

In a large pot over low heat, sauté the garlic and onion in the olive oil. When onions begin to brown, stir in the chicken stock and rice. Add the tomatoes while continuing to stir. Add the seasonings, continue stirring, then add the shrimp. Mix well and transfer to a $2^{1}/_{2}$ to 3-quart baking dish coated with olive oil.

Bake, covered, for about 1 hour or until the rice is thoroughly cooked.

Remove cover and bake for an additional 10 to 15 minutes until the top begins to brown slightly.

Baked Scallops and Shells

FILE UNDER: **Not So Bad for You**

In addition to loving cheese, I'm a little cheesy. That's why, when making a seafood casserole, I like to use shell pasta. You absolutely don't have to do this, but they do go so well together. I've only ever made this with fresh scallops, but frozen and thawed should suffice.

SERVES 4 TO 5

1/2 pound medium shell pasta

1 large white onion, chopped

3 cloves garlic, minced or pressed

5 tablespoons butter

1 pound large fresh scallops

Salt and pepper to taste

1 cup grated or shredded Parmesan cheese

3/4 cup half-and-half or whole milk

2 teaspoons chopped fresh parsley

1/4 cup bread crumbs

Preheat oven to 375°F.

In a large pot of salted water, cook the pasta until just under al dente. Drain and set aside.

In a large pan over medium heat, sauté the onions and garlic in 2 tablespoons of the butter until the onions are translucent. Add the scallops and 2 more tablespoons of the butter. Season with salt and pepper. Stir constantly until the scallops are lightly browned.

In a large bowl, mix the shells, Parmesan, milk, and parsley. When the pasta is coated, salt and pepper to taste, and add the scallops, onion, and garlic. Mix well and transfer to a 2½-quart greased or buttered casserole dish.

Bake, uncovered, 25 to 30 minutes, or until bubbly.

In a small bowl, mix the bread crumbs with 1 tablespoon of softened butter. When the casserole is bubbly, remove from oven and top with the bread crumb and butter mixture. Bake approximately 10 more minutes or until the bread crumbs are golden brown.

Let stand 5 minutes before serving.

Creamy Mushroom-Risotto Casserole

Similar to a recipe that won first place at my Second Annual Casserole Party, this mushroom-risotto casserole is a little easier and incorporates fewer and easier-to-find ingredients. This is a rather brown dish, and the sweet peas give it much-needed color. This dish can be made vegetarian with a vegetable broth or stock.　　　　SERVES 6 TO 7

4 tablespoons butter

2 tablespoons extra-virgin olive oil

2 cups Arborio rice

5 to 6 cups chicken stock or low-sodium chicken broth

1 to 2 teaspoons salt

Freshly ground black pepper

1 large white onion, chopped

2 pounds white button or baby portobello mushrooms, cleaned and chopped

3 cloves garlic, minced or pressed

1 tablespoon soy sauce

3 tablespoons chopped fresh parsley

1 cup heavy cream

1½ cups freshly grated Parmesan cheese

16 ounces frozen sweet peas

2 large eggs, lightly beaten

In a large saucepan over medium heat, melt 2 tablespoons of the butter with the olive oil. Add the rice, stirring frequently until the rice is coated. Add two cups of the chicken broth and a teaspoon each of salt and pepper. Continue to stir so the rice does not stick to the bottom of the pan. Once the broth is absorbed, add more broth, a half cup to a cup at a time until the rice is tender. This should take 15 to 20 minutes. You may end up only using 4 to 5 cups of the broth. This is okay, and it's fine if your rice is a little soupy (you're going to bake it!). Salt and pepper and remove the pan from the heat.

In a separate pan, melt the remaining butter over medium heat. Once the butter is melted, add the onions. Use more olive oil or butter, if needed, so that the onions don't stick to the pan. When the onions become translucent, reduce the heat to low and add the mushrooms and garlic. After about 2 minutes, add the soy sauce and parsley and stir. Cook over low heat for 2 to 3 minutes, stirring occasionally, then add the heavy cream. After about 1 minute, transfer mixture to the rice, add 1 cup of the Parmesan, and stir until thoroughly mixed. Salt and pepper to taste and add the peas (they can, and should, go in frozen).

Transfer to a greased or buttered 9 × 13-inch baking dish. Pour the two eggs over the top, coating the mixture evenly, and sprinkle ¼ cup (about half of what you have left) of the Parmesan on top of the eggs, again coating evenly. Sprinkle pepper on top.

Bake, uncovered, for 30 to 35 minutes or until the top begins to brown. Remove from oven, sprinkle the rest of the Parmesan on top, and bake for an additional 10 minutes.

Let stand 10 minutes before serving.

Paula Deen's Crab and Spinach Casserole

FILE UNDER: Oh So Good but Bad for You

I like to pretend that anything that has spinach in it is healthy. It's one of the lies I tell myself and why I always have a spinach salad when I'm eating macaroni and cheese; I feel in some way I'm counteracting the calories and fat. I'm not, and neither is Paula Deen with this crab and spinach casserole that's made rich and delicious the Paula Deen way: with butter, cheese, whole milk ("*Not* 1% or 2%," says Paula.) *and* half-and-half. If you've ever made a Paula Deen recipe, you know the result is always well worth the fact that you'll have to change into your sweatpants before you finish your dinner. And that's the way she intends it to be.

If you're anything like me, this casserole utilizes the rarely touched underbelly of your oven—the broiler!—making the top wonderfully crispy. But it can also be made ahead of time and refrigerated, then baked in the regular part of the oven we all know and love. This can be made in one large serving or in eight individual ramekins. SERVES 8

2 (10 ounce) packages frozen leaf spinach, thawed and drained

1 stick butter

1 clove garlic, minced

2 tablespoons grated yellow onion

$1/3$ cup all-purpose flour

3 cups whole milk

1 cup grated Swiss cheese

1 cup half-and-half

2 teaspoons fresh lemon juice

Pinch garlic powder

Dash freshly grated nutmeg

1 teaspoon salt

$1/4$ teaspoon cayenne pepper

2 pounds fresh crabmeat, picked through twice for shells

1 cup fresh bread crumbs

Preheat the broiler. Butter a shallow 2-quart baking dish or 8 ovenproof individual ramekins.

In a 12-inch skillet over medium heat, sauté the spinach in 2 tablespoons of the butter with the garlic and onion for 3 minutes. Drain the spinach mixture and chop finely. Transfer the spinach to the baking dish.

In a large saucepan over medium heat, melt 4 tablespoons of the butter. Stir in the flour and whisk until smooth. Reduce the heat to low and gradually add the milk, stirring constantly with a spoon until smooth and thickened; this should take 8 to 10 minutes. Once the sauce is thickened, add the cheese, half-and-half, lemon juice, garlic powder, nutmeg, salt, and cayenne. Cook over low heat until thickened again, about 10 minutes. Remove the sauce from the heat and carefully fold in the crabmeat.

Pour the mixture evenly over the spinach. Sprinkle with the bread crumbs and dot with the remaining 2 tablespoons of the butter (you may need more bread crumbs if you're preparing individual servings).

Broil about 5 minutes, until browned.

Let stand 5 minutes before serving.

NOTE: If you're making this ahead of time, skip the broiler. After you top the bread crumbs with the butter, cover and refrigerate. When you're ready to cook, uncover and bake for about 30 minutes or until bubbly in a preheated 350°F oven. Then change the oven setting to broil and broil the top for about 5 minutes.

Friday Chicken

FILE UNDER: **Not So Bad for You, Gluten-Free**
(if you use gluten-free broth and soy sauce), Lactose-Free

Every Friday I have friends over to test the casseroles I make and to help me get rid of them. But on a recent Friday I was a little tired of entertaining and decided I would cook up the chicken I was going to put in the casserole I didn't make, and sit by myself and drink wine and watch bad TV. However, this baked chicken with pearl onions was so good, I had to call a friend over to help me eat it.

SERVES 4

2 pounds (about 3 large or 4 medium) boneless, skinless chicken breasts

1 tablespoon salt

1 tablespoon pepper

$1/2$ cup balsamic vinaigrette

$1/2$ cup vegetable broth

$1/2$ cup extra-virgin olive oil

$1/4$ cup soy sauce

1 tablespoon cayenne pepper

2 cloves garlic, sliced

$1/2$ cup chopped green onions

1 cup pearl onions

Arrange the chicken breasts in a shallow 8 or 9-inch-square baking dish. Rub the chicken breasts with the salt and pepper, then pour the vinaigrette, broth, olive oil, and soy sauce over them (no need to mix first, but you can if you want). Flip the breasts over in the marinade a few times.

Sprinkle the cayenne pepper, garlic, and green onions on top of the chicken, then arrange the pearl onions around the chicken breasts.

Cover and refrigerate for at least 3 hours.

Bake, uncovered, at 400°F for about 1 hour and 15 minutes or until done.

For best results, baste at least once while baking.

Easy Cheesy Chicken Enchiladas

This chicken and cheese enchilada recipe is super-easy and cheesy, much like my unfortunate rhyme. As usual, I've added some cayenne for kick, but if you like your Mexican food on the mild side, feel free to leave it out. I like to serve these with a dollop of sour cream and a sprinkle of diced, raw white onions. If you're like me, you don't even need a fork, just some tortilla chips (if your enchiladas are soft enough, the chips will cut right through). Or if you're a civilized human being, unlike me, a fork and knife will do just fine.   SERVES 7 TO 8

1 large white onion, chopped

2 cloves garlic, minced

2 to 3 tablespoons olive oil

4 boneless, skinless chicken breast halves

1/2 green bell pepper, chopped

1 (15 ounce) can pureed tomatoes

1 tablespoon chili powder

1/2 teaspoon dried oregano

1/2 teaspoon cayenne pepper

Salt and pepper

1 teaspoon sugar, optional

1/2 pint sour cream

1 1/2 cups shredded cheddar cheese

8 (10 inch) corn or flour tortillas

1 (12 ounce) jar taco sauce

Preheat oven to 350°F.

In a medium skillet (preferably nonstick) over medium heat, sauté the onions and garlic in the olive oil. When the onions begin to cook, add the chicken breasts and green peppers. (You can either cube the chicken before cooking or cube or shred it after cooking. I prefer my chicken shredded, which you can easily do with your hands once it's cooked and cooled.)

Once the chicken is cooked through, add the tomatoes, chili powder, oregano, and cayenne, and stir. Salt and pepper to taste. If the sauce is on the sour side, you can add the sugar. Add the sour cream and 1 cup of the cheddar cheese while continuing to stir.

When the cheese is melted and you have a wonderful gooey mix in your skillet, salt to taste then spoon an even amount of the mixture into each of the 8 tortillas and roll them up. Align in a greased 9×13-inch casserole dish. Cover with taco sauce and the remaining 1/2 cup of the cheddar cheese.

Bake, uncovered, for 20 to 25 minutes or until bubbly.

Let stand 5 to 10 minutes before serving.

Chicken Mole Enchiladas

FILE UNDER: Not So Bad for You

These enchiladas are prepared much like the Easy Cheesy Chicken Enchiladas (page 89), but with a mole sauce. Until putting together this recipe, I thought that mole sauce was a Mexican chocolate sauce. And while mole can, in fact, have Mexican chocolate in it, it doesn't have to. This one does. Make the mole sauce ahead of time, and add half to the chicken mixture. The rest of the sauce goes on top.

SERVES 7 TO 8

Mole Sauce

1 cup finely chopped white or yellow onion

2 cloves garlic, minced or pressed

2 tablespoons vegetable oil

2 (10.75 ounce) cans condensed tomato soup or pureed tomatoes

3 to 4 tablespoons fresh (seeds removed) or 2 (4 ounce) cans diced green chile peppers

2 tablespoons unsweetened cocoa powder

2 teaspoons ground cumin

2 teaspoons chopped fresh cilantro

$1/2$ teaspoon cayenne pepper

In a saucepan over medium heat, sauté the onions and garlic in the vegetable oil. Add the tomato soup, green chile peppers, cocoa powder, and spices. Bring sauce to a boil, stir well, and reduce the heat to low. Cover and let simmer for 15 to 20 minutes, stirring occasionally. Remote from heat and set aside.

Enchiladas

1 large white onion, chopped

2 cloves garlic, minced

2 to 3 tablespoons olive oil

4 boneless, skinless chicken breast halves

$1/2$ can (8 ounces) pureed tomatoes

1 tablespoon chili powder

$1/2$ teaspoon dried oregano

$1/2$ teaspoon cayenne pepper

Salt and pepper

$1/2$ of the prepared mole sauce

$1/2$ pint sour cream

8 (10 inch) corn or flour tortillas

Preheat oven to 350°F.

In a medium skillet (preferably nonstick) over medium heat, sauté the onions and garlic in the olive oil. When the onions begin to cook, add the chicken breasts. (You can either cube the chicken before cooking or cube or shred it after cooking. I prefer my chicken shredded, which you can easily do with your hands once it's cooked and cooled.)

Once the chicken is cooked through, add the tomatoes, chili powder, oregano, and cayenne, and stir. Salt and pepper to taste. When fully mixed, add the mole sauce and sour cream while continuing to stir.

Once you have a wonderful gooey mix in your skillet, salt to taste then spoon an even amount of the mixture into each of the 8 tortillas and roll them up. Align in a greased 9 × 13-inch casserole dish. Cover with the remaining mole sauce.

Bake, uncovered, for 20 to 25 minutes or until bubbly.

Let stand 5 to 10 minutes before serving.

Vegan Tex-Mex Macaroni Casserole

FILE UNDER: Not So Bad for You, Lactose-Free, Vegan, Vegetarian

This casserole, courtesy of Kristen Wright and La Neal, took third place at my Second Annual Casserole Party. Most party-goers had no clue that it was vegan because the ingredients were so good. And yes, Fritos are vegan. Who knew? While the brands suggested make a mean vegan casserole I can vouch for, feel free to substitute your own favorite brands of vegan meat, cheese, and sour cream. SERVES 6

1/2 pound elbow macaroni

1 medium red onion, chopped

2 garlic cloves, minced or pressed

2 tablespoons canola oil

1 package (3/4 pound) Yves Veggie Cuisine Veggie Ground Round Mexican

Salt and pepper to taste

1/2 brick Vegan Gourmet Monterey Jack cheese, grated or cubed

1 pound Vegan Gourmet Cheddar, shredded

5 spring onions, chopped

8 ounces frozen whole-kernel corn

1 (15 ounce) can black beans, partially drained

1 (14.5 ounce) can diced tomatoes with juice

1 (8.9 ounce) can sliced black olives, drained

3/4 to 1 cup Tofutti Sour Supreme

1 to 2 cups Fritos corn chips

Preheat oven to 350°F.

In a large pot of salted water over medium heat, cook the macaroni to just under al dente. Drain and set aside.

In a large pan over medium heat, sauté the onions and garlic in the canola oil. After 3 to 5 minutes, or when the onions begin to cook, add the Veggie Ground Round. Add salt and pepper to taste and cook, stirring, until hot.

Add the Monterey Jack and cover the pan, but keep a close eye, stirring at least every two minutes, until the cheese is melted. Because you're working with vegan ingredients, you may need to sprinkle a little water in the pan to keep the "cheese" from burning and sticking, but don't turn down the heat, or it won't cook at all.

In a large pot over low heat, mix the remaining ingredients except the Fritos with the contents of your frying pan. Salt and pepper to taste. Transfer to a 2½-quart baking dish. Bake, uncovered, for 20 to 30 minutes until the cheese is melted and the liquid is bubbling.

Sprinkle with crushed Fritos and serve.

A Kansas City Masterpiece

I'm from a suburb of Kansas City, Missouri. And if there's one thing Kansas City does better than any other place in the country, it's barbeque sauce, and KC Masterpiece is one of my favorites. After I moved to New York at eighteen, I was justifiably homesick. My first apartment was a dark studio in the basement of an orthodox Jewish family's home in Midwood, Brooklyn. I remember strolling the aisles of the local grocery, weeping because I couldn't find KC Masterpiece sauce, something that had been so ubiquitous in my previous life.

One teary-eyed phone call later, relatives were shipping me the sauce. When the first box arrived, I ripped it open and immediately went to my kitchenette to find something to use it with. I had some penne pasta and cheese and, miraculously, some chicken in the freezer (a rare occurrence). I quickly threw together a remedial version of the recipe below and have since found that most grocers in New York (that aren't specialty Jewish shops) do, in fact, carry KC Masterpiece barbeque sauce. If you can't find KC Masterpiece, any old sauce will do. But at least try to find one that's thick and sweet, as opposed to runny and vinegar heavy.

SERVES 6 TO 7

1 pound penne pasta

1 large white onion, finely chopped

1 clove garlic, finely chopped

1/4 cup olive oil

2 cups (about 3/4 pound) chopped boneless, skinless chicken breast

1 cup KC Masterpiece Hot & Spicy BBQ Sauce

1/2 pound Monterey Jack cheese, cubed

1 (15 ounce) can black beans, drained

Salt and pepper to taste

1/2 cup sour cream

1/2 cup finely chopped chives

Preheat oven to 350°F.

In a large pot of salted water, cook the penne to just under al dente. Drain and set aside.

In the bottom of the same large pot, over high heat, sauté the onion and garlic in the olive oil until the onion becomes translucent. Add the chicken to the pot and cook until done.

Reduce the heat to low. Add the barbeque sauce and cheese and stir. Add the pasta and black beans and mix until the pasta is completely coated with the sauce. Salt and pepper to taste.

Transfer to a lightly greased or buttered 2½ to 2¾-quart baking dish and bake for 45 minutes or until bubbly.

Remove from the oven and let cool for 10 minutes before serving. Add a dollop of sour cream and a sprinkle of chives on top of each serving.

Thanksgiving Casserole

Since I moved to New York in 2000, I've been a Thanksgiving orphan. I go home to Missouri for Christmas, so it doesn't make too much sense to go home at Thanksgiving as well. Luckily for me, many of my friends are in the same boat, so I often host Thanksgiving at my apartment. And year after year, no matter how much my friends and I like to eat, there's always leftover turkey. The casseroles and stuffing tend to go first, maybe because we all like carbohydrates a little too much. This turkey and stuffing casserole is a great way to use leftover turkey, and is written assuming everything else has disappeared. To really make it taste like Thanksgiving dinner, add a cup of dried cranberries. Feel free to leave them out if you'd like a completely savory dish.

SERVES 8

1 (10.75 ounce) can cream of mushroom soup

1 (8 ounce) carton sour cream

1 stick butter, melted

1½ cups chicken or vegetable broth

4 cups Stove Top or other dried stuffing mix

6 cups turkey, shredded

1 cup dried cranberries, or "craisins"

1 cup finely chopped celery

Salt and pepper to taste

Preheat oven to 350°F.

In a large bowl, mix the cream of mushroom soup, sour cream, melted butter, and broth. Add the dried stuffing and mix well. Add the turkey, cranberries, and celery and mix well. Salt and pepper to taste. Depending on your choice of stuffing, this dish may or may not need salt and pepper. Transfer to a greased or buttered 2½ to 2¾-quart baking dish.

Bake, uncovered, for 35 to 45 minutes or until the casserole is brown on top and bubbly throughout.

Let stand 5 minutes before serving.

Tater Tot Turkey Casserole

All I have to say about this casserole is, don't knock it until you try it. If you're from Kansas, you already know how good this dish is. If you're not, I think you're going to be pleasantly surprised. Also great for third-graders. Or for feeling like you're in third grade again. You know, with beer. Courtesy of Apryl Mathes, a Kansas native.   SERVES 4

½ cup celery slices

1 tablespoon olive oil

1 pound ground turkey

½ clove garlic, crushed or minced

1 (10.5 ounce) can cream of mushroom soup

4 cups frozen tater tots

Preheat oven to 350°F.

In a medium pan, sauté the celery in the olive oil over low heat until softened. Add the turkey and garlic. When the turkey is cooked through, add the mushroom soup.

Transfer the whole concoction to a greased 1½ to 2-quart casserole dish. Add the tater tots on top (Apryl suggests placing them vertically so you get more tots in each savory bite).

Bake, uncovered, for 40 to 45 minutes.

Serve with a delightfully tacky cheap beer.

Scalloped Oysters

FILE UNDER: Oh So Good but Bad for You

This is another one of those "don't knock it till you try it" delightfully tacky dishes. It's courtesy of my roommate Maria Flores (well, really her grandmother), who swears by it. The original recipe didn't call for onion, but I added it anyway, because by now you know how I feel about onions.

SERVES 4 TO 5

1½ sleeves Ritz crackers, crushed

1½ sticks butter, melted

1 pint shucked oysters

½ large white onion, finely chopped

½ cup half-and-half or light cream

½ teaspoon salt

½ teaspoon pepper

Preheat oven to 350°F.

In a mixing bowl, combine the crushed Ritz crackers and melted butter. Spread a third of the mixture in the bottom of a round 2 to 2½-quart casserole dish. Cover with half of the oysters, half of the onions, and another third of the cracker mixture. Add the rest of the oysters and the remaining onions.

In a small bowl, mix the cream, salt, and pepper and pour over the casserole. Top with the remaining cracker mixture and bake, uncovered, for 40 to 45 minutes.

FILE UNDER: **Not So Bad for You**

I'm not going to lie—this simple, old-school recipe is one step up from tuna noodle casserole. However, it can pass as a sophisticated baked salmon dish if it's served on fancy dishes with white wine. If you don't want to bother with cooking two salmon steaks, canned salmon will do. Again, my cheesiness shines through—pairing seafood with shell pasta. If you don't want to use shells, use whatever pasta you'd like, though something on the small side works better in this dish than something like linguini.

SERVES 6 TO 7

1 pound medium shell pasta

1 large white onion, chopped

2 to 3 tablespoons olive oil

4 cups milk

6 tablespoons all-purpose flour

Zest and juice of 1 lemon

Salt and pepper to taste

1 (16 ounce) bag frozen sweet peas

2 cups sliced baby portobello mushrooms

1 to 2 teaspoons chopped fresh dill weed or parsley, optional

2 (8 ounce) salmon steaks, cooked and flaked

Preheat oven to 350°F.

Cook the shells in a large pot of salted water to just before al dente. Drain and set aside.

In the same large pot over medium heat, sauté the onions in the olive oil for 4 to 5 minutes. Add the milk and flour and stir continuously. When the mixture is smooth, add the lemon zest, salt, and pepper. Stir. As the sauce begins to thicken, add the pasta and stir. When the pasta is coated, add the peas, mushrooms, dill or parsley, lemon juice, and salmon. Salt and pepper to taste.

Transfer to a 2³/₄ to 3-quart baking dish and bake, uncovered, for 45 minutes or until bubbly throughout.

Let stand 5 minutes before serving.

Classic Meat Loaf

A dish so good a rock star named himself after it, the meat loaf is a ubiquitous Midwestern dinner on the cheap. When I was a kid, it was always served with green beans, mashed potatoes, and lots of ketchup. This flavorful loaf with a ground beef and bread crumb base, however, doesn't require any extra ketchup.

TIP: Line the bottom of your baking dish with bread. It will soak up all the grease and fat and you can throw it away after baking. If you don't want the grease, that is.   SERVES 4 TO 6

½ cup ketchup

⅓ cup brown sugar

1 tablespoon balsamic vinegar

1 teaspoon Dijon mustard

2 pounds lean ground beef

3 slices bread, crumbled, ort 1¼ cups bread crumbs

1 large white onion, chopped

2 cloves garlic, minced

2 eggs, beaten

¼ teaspoon cayenne pepper

1 cube beef bouillon, crumbled

3 tablespoons lemon juice

Preheat oven to 350°F.

In a small bowl, combine the ketchup, brown sugar, balsamic vinegar, and mustard until smooth.

In a large bowl, combine ground beef, bread, onion, garlic, eggs, cayenne, bouillon, 3 tablespoons of lemon juice, and ⅓ cup of the ketchup mixture until well mixed. Form into a loaf and place in a 9×5-inch loaf pan.

Bake, uncovered, for about 1 hour. Drain the fat or see the tip for reducing grease above. Cover the loaf with the remaining ketchup mixture and bake, uncovered, for an additional 10 to 15 minutes or until the glaze is set.

Chicken Noodle Souperole

Chicken noodle soup and casseroles are well-known for being American comfort foods. So can you imagine anything in the world more comforting than chicken noodle soup casserole, or Chicken Noodle Souperole? Instead of using a broth, like most soups, this dish incorporates condensed soups, giving it a thicker consistency before it is baked.   SERVES 5 TO 6

4 skinless, boneless chicken breast halves

1 (12 ounce) package egg noodles

1 large white onion, chopped

2 cloves garlic, minced

1/2 cup carrots, chopped

1/2 cup celery, chopped

3 to 4 tablespoons olive oil

1/2 stick of butter

1 (10.75 ounce) can condensed cream of mushroom soup

1 (10.75 ounce) can condensed cream of chicken soup

1/2 cup sour cream

Salt and pepper

1 tablespoon chopped fresh parsley

1 cup crumbled saltines or buttery crackers, optional

Preheat oven to 350°F.

In a large pot of boiling water (with a drizzle of olive oil and a tablespoon of salt), boil the chicken breasts until they are cooked through. Remove the chicken and set aside. In the remaining water, parboil the egg noodles (about 3 to 4 minutes). While the noodles are cooking, cut the chicken into 1/2-inch pieces. Drain the pasta and set aside.

In the same large pot, over low heat, sauté the onion, garlic, carrots, and celery in the olive oil and butter. When the onions begin to appear translucent, add the mushroom soup, chicken soup, and sour cream and mix well. Salt and pepper to taste. Add the noodles and, once they are fully coated, add the chicken pieces and parsley.

Transfer to a greased or buttered 2³/₄-quart baking dish. Bake for 40 to 45 minutes or until bubbly. If you'd like, remove from oven and add crumbled crackers on top. Return to oven for 5 to 10 minutes.

Let stand 5 minutes before serving.

Bubby's Lamb Cobbler

This recipe from Ron Silver, chef and owner of Bubby's Pie Company in New York City, combines savory cheese scones cobbled atop a rich lamb stew. Ron suggests asking your butcher to cut the lamb into large stew-size chunks so you don't have to. This recipe is made in two steps before it goes in the oven: the stew and the savory cheese biscuits, which together make up the cobbler. The stew can be made ahead of time, but the biscuit dough should be made just before the entire dish goes in the oven.

SERVES 6 TO 8

2 pounds lamb shoulder meat cut in large stew-size chunks (1½ to 2 inches)

1 tablespoon salt

1 teaspoon ground black pepper

⅓ cup flour

4 tablespoons butter

1 tablespoon canola oil

3 cups chopped onion

2 cloves garlic, sliced coarse

2 to 3 tablespoons fresh thyme, chopped

1 tablespoon fresh rosemary, stripped off stem and chopped fine

1 cup red wine

1½ cups carrots

1½ cups parsnips

1 cup potatoes, diced in ¼-inch cubes

½ cup celery (or fresh fennel bulb), sliced into ¼-inch pieces

3 cups chicken stock

1 tablespoon butter

1 tablespoon flour

¼ cup chopped fresh parsley

Season the lamb chunks with salt and pepper and toss the lamb in flour. The coating gives it a nice texture when browned, then later lends itself to thicken the stew. In a big sauté pan, heat the butter and oil over medium-high heat. When it's hot and bubbly, add the lamb. Stir and turn it occasionally. When the meat is really browned on all sides, remove it from the pan and set aside. Leave the fond, the brown bits that stick to the bottom of the pan, there and add the onions and garlic. Sauté them until golden brown, stirring occasionally. Add the thyme and rosemary. To deglaze, turn the heat up to medium high, pour in 1 cup of wine, and scrape up the fond into it. When you notice that most of the juices are reduced, transfer everything to a heavy soup pot.

Prepare carrots and parsnips: Peel, chop off tips and stem ends, quarter them lengthwise, and chop the whole batch in ¼ to ½-inch pieces. Slice celery. Scrub the potatoes well and leave the skin on—God put skin on potatoes because it's good. Add the vegetables and lamb to the soup pot and add the chicken stock. Simmer it slow, uncovered, until the liquid reduces by about a third—about an hour and a half or so.

Make a blonde roux: melt 1 tablespoon of butter in a small sauté pan over medium-high heat. Stir in the leftover flour, smashing up any lumps. Continue stirring until the roux has an even consistency and is runny and bubbly. (Don't scorch it.) Remove from heat. Add the roux to the lamb stew mixture, stirring as you add it. It should have a thick, stewlike consistency. Adjust seasonings and remove from heat. Add the parsley. You can make the dish up to this point 24 hours in advance—it improves in flavor. Or you can make it that day for dinner. The stew doesn't need to cool before the scones are added; in fact, it should be hot. If you are using stew that has been refrigerated, reheat it over medium heat to piping hot before topping with biscuits.

Savory Cheese Biscuits for Lamb Cobbler

3 cups flour

1½ tablespoons baking powder

1½ tablespoons sugar

¼ teaspoon salt

¼ teaspoon cayenne pepper

½ cup sharp white cheddar cheese, grated

1½ cups heavy cream

Heavy cream for the top

Sift together the dry ingredients then stir in the cheddar cheese and add the cream. Pour the hot stew into a 3-quart baking dish and top with 2-tablespoon-size chunks of biscuit dough. Brush the top of the dough cobbles with heavy cream. Bake at 375°F for 30 to 45 minutes or until the biscuits are golden and the stew is bubbling.

Matt Hamilton's Rabbit Casserole

FILE UNDER: Oh So Good but Bad for You

Matt Hamilton, chef of the hip East Village bistro Belcourt, is known for his sophisticated comfort food like boudin blanc sausage disguised as a hot dog and ground lamb burgers with chèvre. His Rabbit Stew Casserole with buttermilk biscuits is comfort food at its most grown-up. This recipe calls for a bouquet garni, which is French for a bundle of herbs usually tied together with string (or tied up in cheesecloth) and often used to enhance the flavors in soups, stocks, and stews. As you'll see in the instructions, the bouquet is boiled with the other ingredients, and removed before serving.   SERVES 4

2 whole rabbits	1 quart turnips, quartered
Salt and pepper	1/4 bunch thyme
Nutmeg	1/4 bunch sage
2 cups rabbit sausage (scraps)	2 quarts chicken stock
2 onions, diced	Bouquet garni of allspice, peppercorns, cinnamon, and cloves
4 carrots, diced	
2 bulbs fennel, diced	Smoked paprika

Remove all the meat from the legs and remove the tender loins. Cut into quarter-size pieces and season with salt, pepper, and nutmeg. All of the other scraps of the rabbit need to be seasoned with salt and pepper and ground in a meat grinder.

Sweat the sausage in olive oil and then add all of the diced vegetables and turnips. When the veggies are tender, add the rest of the rabbit meat and cook through. Add the fresh herbs and cook some more. Then add the chicken stock and the bouquet garni and bring to a boil. Reduce the heat and simmer for about 1/2 hour. Remove and let cool. Wring out the bouquet garni and discard.

Buttermilk Biscuits

3 cups all-purpose flour	2 teaspoons sugar
1 teaspoon salt	1 cup butter
4 teaspoons baking powder	1 1/2 cups buttermilk

Combine all of the dry ingredients. Cut the butter into the dry ingredients with your fingers until it resembles coarse crumbs. Add the buttermilk and, using your hands, combine with the dry ingredients until it is fully incorporated and resembles dough.

Put your rabbit stew into an ovenproof container and top with the biscuit dough. Bake at 400°F until the biscuits are golden brown. Dust with the smoked paprika.

Lemon Chicken and Rice

FILE UNDER: Not So Bad for You, Gluten-Free, Lactose-Free

Similar to a recipe my mom used to make with instant rice and juice out of a plastic lemon, this lemon chicken and rice casserole requires no stove-top preparation and is a great light summer meal. I like to use a large covered dish for this so I can just mix everything in the dish before it goes into the oven. This recipe makes for a very lemony-tasting meal, so if you'd like the flavor to be less intense, use the juice of two lemons and the zest of one.   SERVES 4 TO 5

1 large white onion, chopped

3 cloves garlic, minced or pressed

1 teaspoon old-style Dijon mustard

1/4 cup olive oil

Zest of 2 lemons

1 cup vegetable broth

1 cup parboiled long-grain rice

1 pound uncooked chicken breast, cut into 1/2-inch pieces

Salt and freshly ground pepper to taste

Juice of 4 lemons, lemons reserved

Preheat oven to 400°F.

Place the onion, garlic, mustard, olive oil, lemon zest, and vegetable broth in a 2 1/2-quart or larger casserole dish. Mix well, then add the rice. When the rice is fully coated, add the chicken and a pinch of salt and pepper. Mix well again. Pour the lemon juice over the mixture, slice 2 of the lemons you reserved from the juice and lay them decoratively on top of the casserole. Sprinkle with freshly ground pepper, and bake, covered, for 1 hour.

After 1 hour, remove the cover and bake an additional 15 minutes.

Let stand 10 minutes before serving.

Tuna and Potato Casserole with Sweet Peas

FILE UNDER: Not So Bad for You

This is one of those recipes I like to call "delightfully tacky." It's one of the few casseroles I make without cheese, so it's not terribly bad for you. Although it's not terribly good for you, either, since it calls for sour cream and butter. To save time, slice your potatoes before you boil them. They'll cook much quicker, so make sure they don't get too mushy.　　SERVES 4 TO 5

2 large white onions, chopped

3 cloves garlic, minced or pressed

6 tablespoons butter

2 to 3 tablespoons olive oil

1 (16 ounce) carton sour cream

Juice of one lemon

$1/2$ teaspoon cayenne pepper

1 teaspoon salt

1 teaspoon pepper

1 (12 ounce) can solid white albacore tuna, drained

1 (16 ounce) package frozen sweet peas

6 medium baking potatoes, peeled, boiled, and cut into 1-inch cubes

Preheat oven to 350°F.

In a skillet over medium heat, sauté the onions and garlic in the butter and olive oil until the onions are translucent. Remove from heat.

In a large bowl, mix the sour cream, lemon juice, and the warm butter, garlic, and onion mixture (pour carefully, it's hot!). Mix well, then add the cayenne, salt, and pepper. Mix well and add the tuna and peas while continuing to stir. Slowly add the potatoes, coating as many as possible.

Transfer to a buttered 2 to $2^{1}/_{2}$-quart baking dish. Bake, uncovered, for 40 to 50 minutes or until golden brown on top.

Donatella Arpaia's Fusilli Al Forno

FILE UNDER: Oh So Good but Bad for You

Restaurateur and entertaining expert Donatella Arpaia is famous for her popular Manhattan restaurants and elegant, no-frills Italian cuisine. This fusilli al forno, or baked pasta, with sweet Italian sausage, shiitake mushrooms, and fresh spinach is no exception. Most of the cooking is done on the stove top, and the dish is transferred to the oven for baking.

SERVES 5 TO 6

1 pound fusilli pasta

2 tablespoons extra-virgin olive oil

1 pound sweet Italian sausage, casing removed

1 medium onion, coarsely chopped

$^1/_2$ pound fresh shiitake mushrooms, cleaned and sliced

2 cups whole milk

2 tablespoons butter

$^1/_4$ cup flour

Salt and pepper

Nutmeg

$^1/_4$ pound fresh spinach, washed and coarsely chopped

1 cup freshly grated Pecorino Romano

$^1/_2$ cup seasoned bread crumbs

Preheat oven to 350°F.

Bring pot of salted water to a rolling boil. Cook the pasta 2 minutes less than the package instructions, drain, and set aside.

Place 1 tablespoon of the olive oil in a large pan on medium heat and brown the sausage until cooked. Remove the sausage and add the onions to the same pan. When the onions become translucent, add the shiitake mushrooms and sauté for about 3 minutes. Remove the mushrooms with a slotted spoon or tongs (the mushroom slices should still be pretty large), and set aside.

Put the milk in a small pan and warm it (do not boil). In another pan, melt the butter, then add the flour and cook for about 3 minutes over medium-low heat, whisking constantly. Then add the warm milk and continuously whisk until all the milk is incorporated. Keep stirring until the sauce thickens, then season with salt, pepper, and nutmeg to taste. Place the sauce into a large mixing bowl, then add the pasta, sausage, onions, mushrooms, spinach, and cheese (except for 2 tablespoons), and toss all together.

Transfer to a buttered 9×9-inch dish. Mix the bread crumbs with the 2 tablespoons of Romano and remaining oil, and sprinkle over the pasta. Bake, uncovered, for 50 minutes or until bubbly.

Let stand 5 minutes and serve.

Chicken and Artichoke Casserole

FILE UNDER: Oh So Good but Bad for You

This casserole is a little on the tart side. It's probably something I would have choked down as a kid, but now I love it with a glass of white wine and a side salad with a sweet vinaigrette dressing to counteract the tartness of the dish.

TIP: Be sure to wipe the mushrooms, instead of washing them, because mushrooms are like sponges and they'll soak up water and later release it into the casserole. SERVES 4 TO 5

1 large white onion, chopped

2 cloves garlic, minced

2 tablespoons olive oil

1 pound chicken breast, cubed

1/2 teaspoon chili powder

Salt and pepper

2 cups finely chopped baby portobello mushrooms

1 cup vegetable broth

1 large egg

1/8 cup cider vinegar

1 teaspoon Dijon mustard

1 cup shredded (about 1/4 pound) cheddar cheese

1 cup grated Parmesan cheese

1 (13.75 ounce) can artichoke hearts, drained and chopped

Preheat oven to 350°F.

In a skillet or large pan over medium heat, sauté the onion and garlic in the olive oil. When the onions become translucent, add the cubed chicken. When the chicken is no longer pink, add half of the chili powder and the salt and pepper to taste. Add the mushrooms and vegetable broth, stir, and let simmer for 5 minutes, stirring occasionally.

In a mixing bowl, combine the egg with the cider vinegar, mustard, and a pinch of salt and pepper. Mix well, then add the cheeses and artichokes. When thoroughly mixed, add the chicken and onions. Stir and transfer to a greased or buttered 2½-quart baking dish.

Bake, uncovered, 50 minutes to 1 hour or until bubbly and golden on top.

Spinach and Spicy Chorizo with Penne

This is one of my favorite casseroles because it incorporates everything I love: spice, meat, pasta, cheese, and a little something green. Make sure you drain all the liquid from your spinach after thawing it. After cooking the chorizo, however, there's no need to blot or drain the grease if there is any. This is not a casserole that really sticks together, but rather wonderfully falls apart on your plate.

SERVES 6

1 pound penne

1 large white onion, chopped

1 to 2 tablespoons olive oil

1 pound spicy chorizo, cut into $1/2$-inch pieces

1 cup chicken broth

Salt and pepper

$1^{1}/_{2}$ cups heavy cream

20 ounces frozen chopped spinach, thawed and drained

1 cup cleaned and chopped baby portobello mushrooms

$1^{1}/_{4}$ cups Parmesan, shredded

Preheat oven to 350°F.

In a large pot of salted water, cook the penne to just under al dente. Drain and set aside.

In the same pot, over medium heat, sauté the onions in the olive oil until they are translucent. Add the chorizo and sauté for an additional 1 to 2 minutes. When the chorizo begins to brown around the edges, add the chicken broth and a dash of salt and pepper. When the broth begins to simmer, add the cream and reduce the heat to low. Mix well, and add the spinach, mushrooms, 1 cup of Parmesan, and another dash of salt and pepper. Let simmer for about 5 minutes, stirring occasionally. Add the pasta and mix until the pasta is fully coated.

Transfer to a lightly greased $2^{3}/_{4}$ to 3-quart casserole dish. Sprinkle half of the remaining Parmesan on top and bake, uncovered, for 40 to 45 minutes or until bubbly. Remove from the oven, cover with the rest of the Parmesan, and bake an additional 10 minutes.

Let stand 5 to 10 minutes before serving.

Bubby's Tweed Kettle Pie

FILE UNDER: Oh So Good but Bad for You

A second recipe from Ron Silver, chef and owner of Bubby's Pie Company, this Tweed Kettle Pie combines mashed potatoes with cream and chives with tender salmon in a white sauce with baby peas. This recipe is a great way to use leftover poached or baked salmon, but fresh salmon works just fine, too.

SERVES 4

Mashed Potatoes

1½ to 2 pounds Idaho potatoes

3 tablespoons butter

4 tablespoons cream cheese

¼ cup milk

Salt and pepper

¼ cup minced chives (or scallions)

Béchamel Sauce

3 teaspoons butter

3 teaspoons flour

1½ cups milk

Pinch salt

Pinch nutmeg

Pinch clove

½ cup onion, chopped

1 cup petite peas

4 ounces fresh salmon fillet

Salted water

1 teaspoon white vinegar

2 tablespoons fresh parsley, finely chopped

½ cup cheddar cheese, grated

1 tablespoon chives, sliced in ½-inch sticks

Preheat oven to 450°F.

To make the mashed potatoes, cover the potatoes with cold water, salt the water, and bring to a rolling boil. Maintain the rolling boil until the potatoes are cooked through. Peel and mash them with the butter, cream cheese, and milk. Season the mashed potatoes with salt and freshly ground pepper to taste. Stir in the chives. Cool.

To make the béchamel sauce, heat the butter in a heavy pan over low heat, add the flour, and stir to a soft paste. Pour 1½ cups milk in a steady stream, whisking as you pour. Add the salt, nutmeg, and clove. Cook 7 to 8 minutes or until thickened, whisking the entire time. Remove from heat.

In a separate pan, sauté the onions in butter until soft and translucent. Add the onions and peas to the cooked béchamel sauce.

To poach raw salmon, heat water 2 inches deep in a sauté pan and add a little salt and a little vinegar. Bring the water to a simmer and add the salmon. Lay it skin side down in pan. Cook to medium-well done. (Salmon should flake but remain supple, yielding.) Drain, cool, and flake the salmon. Add it to the béchamel sauce, and then add the parsley. Fill a ceramic or glass dish with the salmon béchamel. Top with the mashed potatoes. Top the mashed potatoes with the grated cheese and chive sticks.

Bake, uncovered, for 25 minutes. Serve hot.

Chicken, Cheddar, and Sun-Dried Tomato Casserole

FILE UNDER: Oh So Good but Bad for You

Sun-dried tomatoes can often overpower other flavors when baked into a dish, but when I made a chicken and cheddar casserole that was lacking something, I knew sun-dried tomatoes would make it better. So I cut them into really small pieces, and they made this dish a keeper.

SERVES 4 TO 5

1 large white onion, chopped

2 tablespoons olive oil

1 pound chicken breast, cubed

$1/4$ teaspoon cayenne pepper

Salt and pepper

2 cups finely chopped baby portobello mushrooms

1 large egg

$1/2$ cup chicken broth

8 ounces sun-dried tomatoes, dehydrated and finely chopped

2 cups shredded (about $1/4$ pound) cheddar cheese

Preheat oven to 350°F.

In a skillet or large pan over medium heat, sauté the onions in the olive oil until they are translucent. Add the cubed chicken and cook until the chicken is no longer pink. Add the cayenne pepper and a dash of salt and pepper. Reduce the heat to low and add the mushrooms. Let simmer on low for 2 to 3 minutes, stirring occasionally.

In a mixing bowl, combine the egg with the chicken broth and a pinch of salt and pepper. When thoroughly mixed, add in the chicken and onions. Slowly add the sun-dried tomatoes and all but $1/4$ cup of the cheddar cheese. Stir and transfer to a greased or buttered $2^{1}/_{2}$-quart baking dish. Cover with a light sprinkle of the remaining cheddar cheese, reserving some for the end.

Bake, uncovered, 40 minutes to 1 hour or until bubbly and golden on top. Remove from oven, cover with the remaining cheddar, and bake an additional 10 minutes.

Deconstructed Zucchini Lasagna

FILE UNDER: **Not So Bad for You**

If I'd used different noodles and layered this dish instead of mixing it, I would have ended up with a beef and zucchini lasagna. Play around with layers and use a different pasta if you're so inclined, or mix it up with the rigatoni for a wonderful, gooey bake. The spicy beef mixes well with the mild zucchini, but this is one casserole that does not improve if it's overcooked, unless you like mushy zucchini.

SERVES 5 TO 6

12 ounces rigatoni

1 large yellow or white onion, chopped

3 cloves garlic, minced

2 tablespoons olive oil

3/4 pounds ground sirloin

1/2 teaspoon cumin

1/2 teaspoon chili powder

Salt and pepper

1 (24 ounce) can crushed tomatoes with juice

1 teaspoon crushed red pepper

2 tablespoons fresh basil, chopped

12 ounces ricotta cheese

1/2 large zucchini (about 1 1/2 cups sliced and quartered)

1 cup Parmesan cheese

Preheat oven to 350°F.

In a large pot, parboil the rigatoni, drain, and set aside.

In the same large pot, sauté the onions and garlic in the olive oil until the onions are translucent. Add the beef and season with the cumin, chili powder, salt, and pepper. When the meat is browned, add the crushed tomatoes. Mix in the crushed red pepper and basil, and season with salt and pepper as needed. Add the pasta, ricotta, zucchini, and all but 1/4 cup of the Parmesan. Mix well.

Transfer to a 2 3/4-quart baking dish and evenly distribute the remaining Parmesan on top of the casserole.

Bake, uncovered, for 45 minutes. It's important not to overcook this dish, or the zucchini will become soggy.

Chili-Cheese Corn Dog Casserole

After a series of unfortunate events in my last apartment, I had to unexpectedly move out and found myself homeless and staying on friends' couches for a month. I compensated my hosts by making them casseroles. Liz, being one of my regular testers and dinner guests, had already had her fill of all my favorite dishes and called one day on her way home from work to tell me she was craving corn. I had been craving chili so I made this chili-cheese corn dog casserole.

I made my own chili with sweet corn. The recipe is below, but if you'd rather substitute a few cans of prepared chili, you can do that, too. The proportions aren't incredibly important in this dish, as long as you have the five main layers: corn bread, hot dogs, onions, chili, and cheddar cheese. I like to serve it with a handful of chopped raw white onions on top.

SERVES 6 TO 8

2 (8.5 ounce) boxes Jiffy corn muffin mix

2 eggs

2 cups milk

1 large white onion, chopped

1 garlic clove, minced

2 to 3 tablespoons olive oil

1 pound ground beef

1 packet chili seasoning

1 (16 ounce) can tomato paste

2 cups water

1 (15 ounce) can red beans, drained

1 (15 ounce) can black beans, drained

1 (10 ounce) box frozen sweet corn

Cayenne pepper

Salt and pepper

1 pound all-beef hot dogs, cut into ½-inch slices

2 cups finely chopped white onions

1 cup shredded cheddar cheese

Preheat oven to 350°F.

In a large mixing bowl, prepare both boxes of the muffin mix according to the directions on the box (with the eggs and milk). Pour into a buttered 9×13-inch baking dish. Bake only 5 minutes or until it begins to solidify. Remove from oven and let cool.

In a large pot over medium heat, sauté the onions and garlic in the olive oil until the onions become translucent. Add the beef and chili seasoning and cook until the beef is cooked through. Add the tomato paste and water (fill the tomato paste cans with water to get the remaining paste out of the can, and use that water). Mix well and add the beans, stirring constantly (if not, the beans will stick to the bottom). Add the corn, mix, and let simmer for 15 to 20 minutes on low heat, stirring frequently. Add cayenne, salt, and pepper to taste. If the chili has too much bite, feel free to add a few pinches of sugar.

On top of the corn bread, layer the hot dogs, raw chopped onions, chili, cheese, and then another sprinkle of onions.

Bake, uncovered, for approximately 40 minutes or until bubbly, but keep an eye so the corn bread doesn't get too brown. You don't want it to burn.

Let stand 5 minutes before serving.

Julie Powell's Tamale Casserole

FILE UNDER: Oh So Good but Bad for You, Gluten-Free (depending on the tamales)

Inspired by a recipe at the Central Market in Austin, Texas, this is Julie Powell's Tamale Casserole. The trick is finding the tamales premade. If you're not in Austin, you might find them in a Latin market or, if you're lucky, from a street vendor. You'll need 24 of them, cooked.

SERVES 10 TO 12

24 cooked beef and/or pork tamales

1½ cups grated cheddar cheese

1½ cups grated mozzarella cheese

1½ cups grated Monterey Jack cheese

1 (28 ounce) can of Ro-tel or other diced tomatoes with diced green chiles

2 cups chopped onions

1 teaspoon garlic powder

1 teaspoon dried oregano

1 teaspoon cumin

1 teaspoon dark chili powder

1 to 3 teaspoons kosher salt

Preheat oven to 350°F.

In a large bowl, crumble the tamales by hand into bite-size pieces. (A food processor won't work for this.) Toss all remaining ingredients together and add to the tamales.

Transfer to a large greased baking pan or two 9-inch ovenproof dishes and bake, uncovered, for 20 to 30 minutes, until brown and hot throughout.

Aunt Susie's Classic Tuna Noodle Casserole

FILE UNDER: **Not So Bad for You** (save the sodium from the French-fried onions)

As I mentioned in the introduction, this version of the classic tuna noodle casserole is my aunt Susie's. Her secret ingredient is the Salsa Con Queso Cheez Whiz, but if you're just not willing to go there, Parmesan will do just fine. Or skip the cheese altogether. A "real" classic tuna noodle casserole doesn't call for any cheese.

This recipe wouldn't be complete without a crusty topping, so whether you choose potato chips, French-fried onions, or something new, for the love of all things sacred (and yes, this dish is sacred), put something crunchy on top. SERVES 5 TO 6

1 (12 ounce) bag of egg noodles

1 (16 ounce) can cream of mushroom soup

1/2 cup Parmesan cheese or Salsa Con Queso Cheez Whiz

2 (6 ounce) cans white albacore tuna, drained

1 large white onion, chopped

1 (16 ounce) package frozen sweet peas

Salt and pepper

2 cups French-fried onions or a few handfuls of crushed potato chips

Preheat oven to 375°F.

Parboil the noodles just under al dente and drain.

In a large mixing bowl, combine the noodles, soup, cheese, tuna, onions, peas, and salt and pepper to taste. Transfer to a 2½ to 3-quart casserole dish. Bake, uncovered, for 35 to 40 minutes or until bubbling. Remove from oven, add crunchy topping of your choice, and bake for an additional 10 minutes.

Let stand 5 minutes before serving.

Grown-Up Tuna Noodle Casserole

FILE UNDER: Oh So Good but Bad for You

This grown-up casserole incorporates most of the ingredients of a classic tuna noodle casserole. However, I add artichoke hearts and Parmesan cheese and hold the French-fried onions, potato chips, and Cheez Whiz. The tangy artichokes go well with the tuna and Parmesan.

SERVES 5 TO 6

1 (12 ounce) bag of egg noodles

1 (16 ounce) can cream of mushroom soup

1½ cups Parmesan cheese

2 (6 ounce) cans white albacore tuna, drained

1 (16 ounce) package frozen sweet peas

1 (13.75 ounce) can artichoke hearts, drained and chopped

1 large white onion, chopped

Salt and pepper to taste

Preheat oven to 375°F.

Parboil the noodles just under al dente and drain.

In a large mixing bowl, combine the noodles, the soup, 1 cup of the cheese, tuna, peas, artichoke hearts, onion, salt, and pepper. Transfer to a 2½ to 3-quart casserole dish. Bake, uncovered, for 35 to 40 minutes or until bubbling. Remove, top with remaining Parmesan cheese, and bake for an additional 10 to 15 minutes.

Let stand 5 minutes before serving.

FILE UNDER: **Oh So Good but Bad for You**

Like many casseroles, this beefy macaroni with tomatoes and cheese was a result of raiding my own kitchen in a fit of hunger and throwing together what I had on hand (save the Gouda—I ran out for that when I realized it would make the dish complete). I use halved cherry or grape tomatoes (I like the pop of the fresh tomatoes), but if you prefer, pureed or crushed tomatoes will do. If you're in a hurry, this dish doesn't really need to be baked, but it's so much better when it is.   SERVES 6

1 pound elbow macaroni

1 large white onion, finely chopped

2 cloves garlic, minced or pressed

2 tablespoons olive oil

1 pound lean ground sirloin

2 tablespoons cumin

2 tablespoons chili powder

1/2 teaspoon cayenne pepper

Salt and pepper

1/2 pound Gouda, shredded

1/2 pound sharp cheddar cheese, shredded

1 1/2 cups milk

2 cups chopped tomatoes (about 2 medium tomatoes, or use cherry tomatoes, halved)

1 cup cleaned and chopped baby portobello mushrooms

Preheat oven to 350°F.

In a large pot, boil macaroni to just under al dente. Drain and set aside.

In the bottom of the same pot, over medium heat, sauté the onion and garlic in the olive oil until the onions are translucent. Add the ground beef, stirring until it's brown, then add the cumin, chili powder, cayenne, and a dash of freshly ground pepper. Reduce the heat to low and gradually add the pasta, stirring constantly. When the meat and pasta are mixed, gradually add the cheeses while continuing to stir. Mix in the milk, then the tomatoes and mushrooms. Salt and pepper to taste. Stir and transfer to a 2 3/4 to 3-quart baking dish.

Bake, uncovered, for approximately 45 minutes or until cooked through and bubbly.

Reuben Casserole

Much like a Reuben sandwich, this casserole incorporates rye bread, sauerkraut, corned beef, tomato, and Swiss cheese. It's just baked, instead of grilled or toasted. While there are a few stories of the Rueben's origin, its goodness can't be debated. And neither can the goodness of this savory, cheesy casserole.

SERVES 4 TO 6

1 cup mayonnaise

$1/3$ cup Russian or Thousand Island dressing

Salt and freshly ground pepper

4 slices rye bread, cut or torn into 1-inch pieces

2 cups shredded Swiss cheese

1 pound sauerkraut, drained

4 ounces cooked corned beef, thinly sliced

$1^{1}/_{2}$ cups chopped fresh tomatoes

Preheat oven to 350°F.

In a small bowl, mix the mayonnaise, dressing, a pinch of salt, and freshly ground pepper.

Layer half of the bread in the bottom of a buttered 2½-quart casserole dish. Cover the bread with ½ cup of the shredded Swiss cheese, then all of the sauerkraut, corned beef, and dressing. Cover the dressing with 1 cup of the cheese and all of the tomatoes. Cover the tomatoes with the rest of the bread and top the bread with the remaining cheese.

Bake, uncovered, for 25 to 35 minutes or until brown on top and the casserole is hot throughout and just beginning to bubble.

Let stand 5 minutes before serving.

Baked Chili

A little more dense than regular chili, baked chili is about one of the only dishes that makes me long for winter. It's great for Superbowl parties or one of those winter Sundays you spend walking around the house in your long underwear. This can be made either in a Dutch oven and put in the oven, or on the stove top and transferred to a baking dish. **SERVES 6 TO 9**

1½ large white onions, chopped

3 teaspoons olive oil

3 cloves garlic, minced

1 green bell pepper, finely chopped

2 pounds lean ground sirloin

1½ tablespoons chili powder

½ to 1 teaspoon cayenne pepper

1 teaspoon salt

1 teaspoon pepper

1 (28 ounce) can diced tomatoes, with juices

1 (16 ounce) box frozen sweet corn

1 (15 ounce) can kidney beans, drained and rinsed

2 (15 ounce) cans black beans, drained and rinsed

1½ cups shredded cheddar cheese

10 to 15 saltine or butter crackers, crumbled

Sour cream and chives, optional

Preheat oven to 375°F.

In a large pot or Dutch oven over medium heat, sauté the onions in the olive oil until they become translucent. Add the garlic and bell pepper. Sauté for 3 to 5 minutes, then add the sirloin. When the meat is cooked through, add the chili powder, cayenne pepper, salt, and pepper. Mix well, then add the tomatoes, the corn, and the beans. Stir continuously while adding 1 cup of the cheese and the crackers.

If using a Dutch oven, cover and bake for 1 hour or until bubbly. If using a pot, transfer to a 3-quart baking dish, cover, and bake for 45 minutes to 1 hour or until bubbly. Uncover, sprinkle the top of the casserole with the remaining cheese, and bake, uncovered, for 20 to 30 more minutes or until cheese begins to brown on top.

Let stand 5 to 10 minutes, then serve with sour cream and chives.

Kugel with Peas and Onions

FILE UNDER: **Not So Bad for You, Vegetarian**

Most of the kugels I've had in my life are very sweet, so in keeping with that theme while trying to create something on the more savory side, I decided to try my own kugel with caramelized onions and sweet peas. The result is a savory kugel that's still a little sweet. Remember to let the onions caramelize over low heat or you'll end up with crispy black onions, and that's no fun for anyone. The onions really give this dish its flavor. SERVES 6 TO 8

1 pound large egg noodles

4 large onions, finely chopped

3 tablespoons olive oil

7 tablespoons butter, softened

1/2 cup chicken broth

6 large eggs, lightly beaten

Salt and pepper

1 (16 ounce) package frozen sweet peas

Preheat the oven to 375°F.

Cook the egg noodles in boiling salted water, just under al dente. Drain and set aside to cool.

In a skillet over low heat, sauté the onions in the olive oil and 2 tablespoons of the butter. Sauté the onions, stirring frequently, until they are nearly caramelized. This will take about 20 to 30 minutes.

In a large mixing bowl, combine the broth, eggs, and remaining butter. Mix well and add the noodles, ensuring they're all coated. Add the onions and peas, mix well, salt and pepper to taste, and transfer to a greased or buttered 2³/₄ to 3-quart baking dish.

Bake, covered, for 30 minutes then remove the cover and bake another 30 minutes or until the top is golden brown.

Beef and Rice Bake

FILE UNDER: **Not So Bad for You, Gluten-Free (if you use gluten-free beef stock), Lactose-Free**

This simple, hearty dinner is made with ground beef, tomatoes, and long-grain rice. It doesn't call for instant or parboiled rice, so you'll have to pay attention once the dish goes into the oven to make sure you don't under- or overcook the rice. This is a little on the spicy side, so feel free to reduce the amount of cayenne pepper if you don't like your dinner to have too much heat. SERVES 4 TO 5

2 cups uncooked long-grain rice

1 cup beef stock

2 cups water

1 large white onion, finely chopped

1 green bell pepper, finely chopped

3 tablespoons olive oil

1 pound ground sirloin

1 teaspoon chili powder

1 teaspoon cayenne pepper

1 (28 ounce) can pureed tomatoes

Salt and pepper

Preheat oven to 350°F.

Place the rice, beef stock, and water in a large saucepan over medium heat. Bring to a boil, mix well, reduce the heat to low, and let simmer, covered, for 20 minutes or until tender.

In a skillet over medium heat, sauté the onion and green pepper in the olive oil until the onions are translucent. Add the beef, chili powder, and cayenne and cook until the beef is browned. Add the beef mixture to the rice and mix well, then add the pureed tomatoes, and salt and pepper to taste. Transfer to a 2³/₄-quart baking dish, and bake, uncovered, for 40 minutes or until the rice is cooked and the casserole is bubbly.

Beef Stroganoff

This traditional beef casserole calls for skirt steak, which is a little chewy but is one of my favorites, especially when marinated in soy sauce. Use any steak you like, and this dish becomes a great way to get rid of leftovers. You can substitute whole milk for heavy cream.

SERVES 6

12 ounces wide egg noodles

1 large white onion, finely chopped

2 cloves garlic, pressed or minced

2 to 3 tablespoons olive oil

1 pound skirt steak, cut into 1-inch cubes

Salt and pepper

1½ cups heavy cream

1 tablespoon fresh parsley, chopped

2 cups cherry or grape tomatoes, halved

2 cups cleaned and chopped baby portobello mushrooms

1 (16 ounce) bag frozen sweet peas

Preheat oven to 350°F.

In a large pot of boiling salted water, cook the egg noodles just under al dente. Drain and set aside.

In an extra-large pan or large pot over medium heat, sauté the onions and garlic in the olive oil until the onions are translucent. Add the skirt steak and sauté for 2 to 3 minutes, adding about ¼ teaspoon each of salt and pepper. Reduce the heat to low and add the heavy cream. Add the noodles and mix until they're all coated. Add the parsley, tomatoes, mushrooms, and peas. Mix well and transfer to a greased or buttered 2½-quart or larger baking dish.

Bake, uncovered, for 45 minutes or until bubbly.

Let stand 5 minutes before serving.

Pork Chops and Rice

FILE UNDER: Not So Bad for You, Gluten-Free (if you use gluten-free chicken stock), Lactose-Free

These pork chops are browned slightly on the stove before they're transferred to a baking dish to be cooked with rice. You can use brown or white rice, but remember that brown rice takes a little longer to cook than white. Serve these pork chops and rice with a salad and white wine.

SERVES 6

1 cup uncooked rice

2 cups chicken stock

$1/4$ teaspoon salt

$1/4$ teaspoon pepper

6 medium pork chops

1 large white onion, chopped

1 cup sliced baby portobello mushrooms

1 tablespoon chopped fresh parsley

Preheat oven to 350°F.

In the bottom of a lightly greased 9×13-inch baking dish, mix the rice, chicken stock, salt, and pepper.

In a large skillet over medium heat, brown the pork chops (as many as you can fit in the skillet at a time) about 3 to 4 minutes on each side. As the pork chops come out of the skillet, arrange them over the rice in the casserole dish. Bake, covered, for 45 minutes to 1 hour or until the rice is cooked and the pork chops are tender.

While the pork chops and rice are cooking, sauté the onion in the leftover pork chop grease (add a little olive or vegetable oil if needed) until the onions are translucent. Add the mushrooms and sauté for 1 to 2 more minutes. Remove from the heat.

When the rice and pork chops are cooked, remove from the oven, uncover, and pour the onion and mushroom mixture on top. Return the casserole to the oven for 10 to 15 minutes, uncovered.

Remove and sprinkle with the parsley.

Let stand 5 to 10 minutes before serving.

Lactard's Surprise

My friend Mike is lactose intolerant, or "lactarded" as he likes to call it. He asked me to create a casserole for his kind, suggested his favorite ingredients (basil and eggplant), and this is what I came up with. While it would be great with cheese, the egg does a good job of holding the dish together. We sampled it at a few dinner parties and not once did we hear "pass the cheese" from the lactose tolerant in the room. If you don't like spicy beef, reduce the cayenne.

SERVES 4 TO 5

1/2 large eggplant

1/2 pound rotini

1 large white onion, finely chopped

3 cloves garlic, minced or pressed

3 tablespoons olive oil

1 pound ground sirloin

1/2 teaspoon chili powder

1/2 teaspoon cayenne pepper

1/4 teaspoon crushed red pepper

1/2 cup baby portobello mushrooms, chopped

1 (28 ounce) can pureed tomatoes

1/4 cup fresh basil, chopped

3 eggs

1/4 teaspoon salt

1/4 teaspoon pepper

Preheat oven to 350°F.

Slice and quarter the eggplant. Submerge in a bowl of cold salted water for about 15 minutes, then drain.

In a large pot of salted water, cook the rotini to just under al dente. Drain and set aside.

In the bottom of the same large pot, sauté the onions and garlic in the olive oil over medium heat until the onions are translucent. Add the eggplant and sauté for about 3 minutes, then add the beef, chili powder, cayenne, and crushed red pepper. When the beef is cooked through, reduce the heat to low and add the mushrooms, tomatoes, and basil. Mix well, and add the pasta. When the pasta and eggplant are fully coated with the sauce, add 2 lightly beaten eggs. Mix well, and add the salt and pepper. Transfer to a lightly greased 2³/₄-quart casserole dish.

In a small bowl, lightly beat the remaining egg with freshly ground pepper. Pour the egg over the top of the casserole. Bake, uncovered, for 45 to 50 minutes.

Let stand 5 to 10 minutes before serving.

Oven Stew

FILE UNDER: Not So Bad for You, Gluten-Free, Lactose-Free

It's not often that someone comes over, asks what smells so good, and I can claim it's something I've had in the oven all day. But with this easy beef stew, I can. I don't have the counter space for a Crock Pot in my tiny kitchen, so an oven stew is the way to go. But seriously, it takes all day, about eight hours. Feel free to add anything you like, especially root vegetables.

SERVES 4 TO 6

2 pounds beef roast, cubed

6 medium baking potatoes, cubed (skins on!)

1 large white onion, chopped

2 large carrots, sliced

2 turnips, sliced

2 stalks celery, chopped

½ teaspoon chopped fresh cilantro

½ teaspoon chopped fresh parsley

1 teaspoon freshly ground pepper

1 teaspoon salt

1 (16 ounce) can pureed tomatoes

¼ teaspoon sugar

½ teaspoon cayenne pepper

¼ cup water

Preheat oven to 250°F.

Combine all the ingredients in a 4-quart casserole dish, and bake, covered, for about 8 hours.

Hillbilly Stew Casserole

For this recipe, by *hillbilly*, I mean buy a packet of stew seasoning at the grocery store. This simple yet hearty recipe is great for the winter, and you don't have to bother with a Crock Pot. Not that I wouldn't want to bother with a Crock Pot; I would, but there's no room for one in my tiny kitchen.   SERVES 4 TO 6

1 (8 ounce) packet corn muffin mix

1 egg

1 cup milk

1 pound ground beef

1/2 cup water

1 packet of stew mix

1 large white onion, diced

1 cup carrots, diced

2 large baking potatoes, boiled, peeled, and cut into 1-inch pieces

1 (16 ounce) package frozen sweet corn

Preheat oven to 350°F.

Prepare muffin mix according to package instructions with 1 egg and 1 cup of milk. Pour into the bottom of a buttered 9-inch-square casserole dish. Bake for 5 (not 20, like instructed) minutes.

In a large skillet over medium heat, brown the beef, add the water, and season with the stew mix. Mix well and remove the beef with a slotted spoon and distribute evenly over the corn bread. Sauté the onions and carrots in the leftover sauce. When the onions become translucent, add the potatoes and corn. Stir for about 1 minute and pour mixture over the corn bread and beef.

Bake for 20 to 30 minutes or until bubbly.

Classic Lasagna

FILE UNDER: Oh So Good but Bad for You, Vegetarian (optional)

This lasagna is really two recipes in one, depending on whether you choose to make a meat sauce or not. Recipes for both sauces are provided and you can use either for this simple, classic lasagna. The secret is really in the sauce, so your lasagna will only be as flavorful as your sauce. For either option, feel free to add thinly sliced mushrooms, zucchini, and/or fresh spinach in between the layers. This should not affect the cooking time, as all three cook quickly in the oven.

SERVES 8 (VEGETARIAN); 10 (MEAT)

Vegetarian Version

9 lasagna noodles

1 large white onion, chopped

8 cloves garlic, sliced

4 tablespoons olive oil

6 tablespoons chopped fresh basil

2 (28 ounce) cans crushed tomatoes

2 tablespoons dried oregano

1 teaspoon crushed red pepper

1/2 teaspoon salt

1/2 teaspoon pepper

1/2 teaspoon sugar

1 cup red wine

1 (15 ounce) carton ricotta cheese

3 eggs, beaten

1 cup grated Parmesan cheese

1 pound shredded mozzarella cheese

Preheat oven to 350°F.

In a large pot of lightly salted water, cook lasagna noodles to just under al dente (6 to 8 minutes). Drain and set aside.

In the bottom of the same large pot, over medium heat, sauté the onion and garlic in olive oil. When the onions begin to sweat, or become translucent, add half of the basil to the pan and stir, releasing the flavor of the basil into the olive oil. After about 1 minute, add the crushed tomatoes, oregano, crushed red pepper, and another tablespoon of the basil. Reduce heat to low and let simmer for about 30 minutes, stirring occasionally. Add the salt, pepper, sugar, and remaining basil. Mix well, and add additional salt or pepper to taste. Add the red wine, stir, and let simmer an additional 10 minutes.

In a medium bowl, mix the ricotta cheese, eggs, and Parmesan cheese.

Cover the bottom of a lightly greased 9×13-inch baking dish with a thin layer of the sauce, then cover the sauce with three lasagna noodles. Cover the noodles with about 1/4 of the ricotta mixture. Cover the ricotta with about 1/3 of the mozzarella cheese. Then cover the mozzarella with about 1/3 of the remaining sauce. Repeat layers twice more, ending with the mozzarella cheese.

Bake, uncovered, for an hour to an hour and a half or until bubbly, cooked through, and brown on top.

Meat Version

9 lasagna noodles	1 teaspoon crushed red pepper
1 large white onion, chopped	1/2 teaspoon salt
8 cloves garlic, sliced	1/2 teaspoon pepper
4 tablespoons olive oil	1/2 teaspoon sugar
6 tablespoons chopped fresh basil	1 cup red wine
1 pound ground sirloin	1 (15 ounce) carton ricotta cheese
1 teaspoon chili powder	3 eggs, beaten
1/4 teaspoon cayenne pepper	1 cup grated Parmesan cheese
2 (28 ounce) cans crushed tomatoes	1 pound shredded mozzarella cheese
2 tablespoons dried oregano	

Preheat oven to 350°F.

In a large pot of lightly salted water, cook lasagna noodles to just under al dente (6 to 8 minutes). Drain and set aside.

In the bottom of the same large pot, over medium heat, sauté the onion and garlic in the olive oil. When the onions begin to sweat, or become translucent, add half of the basil to the pan and stir, releasing the flavor of the basil into the olive oil. After about 1 minute, add the sirloin, chili powder, and cayenne. When the meat is cooked, add the crushed tomatoes, oregano, crushed red pepper, and another tablespoon of the basil. Reduce the heat to low and let simmer for about 30 minutes, stirring occasionally. Add the salt, pepper, sugar, and remaining basil. Mix well, and add additional salt and pepper to taste. Add the red wine, stir, and let simmer an additional 10 minutes.

In a medium bowl, mix the ricotta cheese, eggs, and Parmesan cheese.

Cover the bottom of a lightly greased 9 × 13-inch baking dish with a thin layer of the sauce, then cover the sauce with three lasagna noodles. Cover the noodles with about ¼ of the ricotta mixture. Cover the ricotta with about ⅓ of the mozzarella cheese. Then cover the mozzarella with about ⅓ of the remaining sauce. Repeat layers twice more, ending with the mozzarella cheese.

Bake, uncovered, for an hour to an hour and a half or until bubbly, cooked through, and brown on top.

Let stand 10 minutes before serving.

Five Ps Italian Casserole

The most important lesson I learned when creating this casserole is that pesto sauce does not bake well. The concentration of olive oil overcooks the basil, so the pesto should be drizzled over the top at the last minute, leaving you to bake four of the five Ps: penne, Parmesan, prosciutto, and peas. This dish can also be made on the stove top. If you choose to do it this way, just sprinkle a little Parmesan and drizzle some pesto on before serving. While it doesn't start with a *P* and, therefore, couldn't be officially included in this dish, halved cherry or grape tomatoes go really well with this.   SERVES 6

1 pound penne pasta

1 large white onion, chopped

2 cloves garlic, minced or pressed

4 to 5 tablespoons olive oil

1½ cups grated or shredded Parmesan cheese

1 (16 ounce) bag frozen sweet peas

¼ pound prosciutto, chopped

Salt and pepper to taste

½ cup fresh or jarred pesto sauce

Preheat oven to 350°F.

In a large pot of salted water, boil the penne to just under al dente. Drain and set aside.

In the bottom of the same pot, over medium heat, sauté the onion and garlic in 2 to 3 tablespoons of the olive oil until the onions are translucent. Reduce the heat to low and add the remaining olive oil and the pasta, mixing well to coat as many of the noodles as you can with olive oil. When the noodles are coated, add the Parmesan cheese, peas, and prosciutto. Salt and pepper to taste. Mix well and transfer to a lightly greased 2½ to 2¾-quart baking dish.

Bake, uncovered, for 35 to 45 minutes then remove and drizzle with the pesto.

Eggplant Casserole

FILE UNDER: Oh So Good but Bad for You, Vegetarian

This spin on eggplant lasagna took best vegetarian dish at my Third Annual Casserole Party. Brooklynite Karol Lu created this recipe especially for the party, and knowing that many people are turned off by the texture of eggplants, she panfried the slices before adding them to a cheesy dish with polenta and tomato sauce. If you're just delving into the world of eggplant, try cutting it into smaller pieces.

SERVES 5 TO 6

2 cups vegetable stock

1 cup cornmeal

3 eggs, beaten, separated

2 tablespoons butter

¾ cup Parmesan cheese

Salt and pepper

1 to 2 tablespoons olive oil

2 eggplants, sliced into ¼ to ½-inch rounds

½ cup ricotta cheese

½ cup half-and-half

2 cups tomato sauce, jarred or homemade

½ pound Fontina cheese, grated

Preheat oven to 375°F.

Begin by making the polenta. Bring vegetable stock to a simmer in a saucepan. Whisk in the cornmeal. Stir continuously with a wooden spoon until mixture thickens. Remove from heat and let cool. Mix in 1 egg (beaten), 2 tablespoons of butter, and ¼ cup Parmesan cheese. Season with salt and pepper, and set aside.

Lightly coat a frying pan with olive oil and heat until almost smoking. Add eggplant, in batches, and fry approximately 3 to 4 minutes on each side. Place finished eggplant slices on a plate with a paper towel to absorb the excess oil.

In a bowl, mix the ricotta cheese, 2 eggs (beaten), half-and-half, and ½ cup Parmesan cheese. Season with salt and pepper.

Lightly brush a 9×13-inch casserole dish with olive oil. Pour in polenta to create the base of the casserole. Add a thin layer of tomato sauce, followed by a layer of eggplant, and a thin layer of the ricotta mixture. Repeat, ending with the sauce. Top with Fontina cheese.

Cover with foil and bake for 40 minutes. Remove foil and broil for 10 minutes or until lightly browned and bubbly on top.

Green Beans and Asparagus with Mozzarella and Tomatoes

FILE UNDER: **Not So Bad for You, Gluten-Free, Vegetarian**

This dish is a fantastic light dinner. Incorporating all fresh, whole ingredients, it's great for summertime with a glass of white wine. There's a little bit of stove-top preparation involved, but beyond blanching the green beans and chopping your ingredients, the oven does most of the work.   SERVES 3 TO 4

2 cups fresh green beans, ends removed and broken in half

1 bunch of asparagus, trimmed and cut into 1-inch pieces

1/4 cup fresh basil, finely chopped

1/2 pound fresh mozzarella, cut into 1/4-inch pieces

1/2 tablespoon olive oil

1/8 teaspoon salt

1/8 teaspoon pepper

1/4 cup freshly grated Parmesan cheese

1 cup cherry tomatoes, halved

Preheat oven to 425°F.

Blanch the green beans and asparagus by cooking them in a large pot of boiling salted water for 2 to 3 minutes. Remove and rinse with cold water to prevent them from cooking further.

In a large mixing bowl, mix the green beans, asparagus, basil, mozzarella, olive oil, salt, and pepper. Transfer to a lightly greased 2-quart casserole dish. Cover with the Parmesan and bake for 35 to 45 minutes.

Cover with the tomatoes and serve.

Carnitas Casserole

This casserole is courtesy of Joanne Phoa and Ben Hagen, who won first-place carnivorous casserole at my Third Annual Casserole Party. Carnitas is a Mexican-style pork confit, and while it may seem complicated, Joanne and Ben walk you through every step below. While preparing the pork is a quite a project and takes a few days, it's well worth the trouble. The "lard" is available at most Mexican groceries. Avoid commercial brands, which are bleached. And free-range pork is suggested.

SERVES 7 TO 8

Carnitas

2½ to 3 pounds boneless pork shoulder or butt (trimmed of excess fat)

Brine (recipe follows)

2 to 3 quarts rendered pork fat "lard"

Orange peel from ½ an orange

3 medium-size poblanos

3 cups salsa verde (recipe follows)

20 corn tortillas

½ pound Monterey Jack cheese with jalapeños, shredded

Tortilla chips, lightly crushed, optional

Radishes, cut into matchsticks, optional

Brine

⅓ cup granulated sugar

½ cup kosher salt

2 tablespoons coriander seeds

2 tablespoons cumin seeds

2 bay leaves

2 cloves

2 chile de arbol

1 onion, sliced

1 carrot, peeled and sliced

6 sprigs cilantro

Two days before serving, trim the pork of excess fat and sinew, and prepare the brine.

For the brine, dissolve the sugar and salt in 2 cups hot water (just hot enough to dissolve the sugar) in a large container. Add 3 quarts very cold water and the rest of the ingredients, and stir to combine.

Place the pork in the brine. Make sure it's completely submerged. Refrigerate for 48 hours.

After 48 hours, remove the pork from the brine. Pat it dry with paper towels and let it stand at room temperature for approximately 1 hour.

Preheat oven to 300°F.

Heat the pork fat in a large Dutch oven over low heat until just warm and melted. Carefully lower the pork into the fat. It should be completely submerged. Add the orange peel to the pork fat. Cook in the oven for 5 to 6 hours, until the meat yields easily when you pierce it with a fork. If the fat starts to boil at any point, turn the oven down to 250°F. When the pork is done, remove it from the oven and let it cool at least 1 hour.

In the meantime, roast the poblanos either on a gas stove or on your outdoor grill. When the poblanos are blackened, place in a bowl with plastic wrap, let them steam for 10 minutes, then remove the skins. Seed and make a small dice.

Carefully take the pork out of the fat. (Strain the fat and store in the freezer if you'd like to make carnitas again.) Break up the pork with your hands into a large bowl. Be sure to remove any sinew that was missed. Mix in the poblanos with the pork. Set aside.

Salsa Verde

(makes 3 cups)
1½ pounds tomatillos

½ cup chopped white onion

½ cup cilantro

1 tbsp fresh lime juice

¼ teaspoon sugar

2 jalapeño peppers, stemmed, seeded, and chopped

kosher salt

For the salsa verde, remove the papery husks from the tomatillos and rinse well. Cut in half and place cut side down on a foil-lined baking sheet. Place under a broiler for about 5 to 7 minutes to lightly blacken the skin.

Place the tomatillos, lime juice, onions, cilantro, jalapeño peppers, and sugar in a food processor (or blender) and pulse until all ingredients are finely chopped and mixed. Salt to taste. Cool in the refrigerator.

Preheat oven to 350°F.

In a large casserole pan (approximately 9×13 inches), layer the pork mixture, salsa verde, and corn tortillas. You can cut the corn tortillas to make them fit. After you've made 3 layers, top with the Monterey Jack cheese and bake until bubbly, approximately 30 to 40 minutes. Remove from the oven, let cool for 5 minutes, and garnish with the tortilla chips and radishes. Serve with slices of avocado and guacamole (homemade of course).

Creamy Mushroom and Onion Pork Chops

FILE UNDER: Oh So Good but Bad for You

This high-protein dinner of pork chops with mushrooms and onions in a creamy sauce is the perfect way to impress a hungry carnivore. Serve with a mixed green salad and a glass of white wine, and your dinner guests will forget that pasta ever existed. Plus, you get to rub garlic cloves on pork chops, which is surprisingly fun!   SERVES 4

4 boneless pork chops (about 2 pounds)

1 whole garlic clove, peeled

Sea salt and freshly ground pepper

2 to 3 tablespoons olive oil

1/4 teaspoon sugar

1 cup sour cream

2 teaspoons Dijon mustard

1/2 teaspoon cayenne pepper

1 large white onion, sliced

1 cup baby portobello mushrooms, cleaned and sliced

1/4 cup white wine

1/4 cup chicken stock

1 1/2 tablespoons flour

1/4 cup chopped fresh parsley

Preheat oven to 350°F.

Rub the pork chops with the garlic clove, then rub salt and pepper into each chop. Chop the garlic.

In a large skillet over medium heat, sauté the pork chops in the olive oil, about 4 to 5 minutes on each side. Remove the pork chops and place them in a lightly greased shallow 8 or 9-inch-square casserole dish. Sprinkle each chop with a pinch of sugar.

In a small bowl, mix the sour cream, mustard, and cayenne.

Add the garlic and onions to the pork chop grease and sauté until the onions are translucent. Add the mushrooms and sauté an additional 1 to 2 minutes. Add the white wine, stock, and flour and mix well. Let simmer for 2 to 3 minutes, stirring occasionally. Slowly add the sour cream mixture, one tablespoon at a time, stirring frequently. When the mixture is smooth, pour over the pork chops, and sprinkle with the parsley and some freshly ground pepper.

Bake, uncovered, 40 to 45 minutes or until bubbly.

Scavenger Casserole

On the Friday before Halloween I left my debit card in one of those machines that sucks it in and gives it back once you finish your transaction. I walked away with my cash, without my card. And I hadn't even begun drinking. I didn't notice until after the bank was closed on Saturday, when I went to buy brunch. I was without currency for a few days, so I did what my early casserole pioneers did and looked around for what I already had in the house and made something wonderful out of it. The result was this spicy shrimp casserole. Luckily, I had a two-pound bag of frozen shrimp in the freezer. If using frozen shrimp, be sure to thaw and remove the tails first! SERVES 6 TO 8

1 pound bow-tie pasta

2 to 3 tablespoons butter

1 medium white or yellow onion, finely chopped

3 cloves garlic, minced or pressed

1 cup milk or half-and-half

2 tablespoons dried oregano

1/2 teaspoon cayenne pepper

2 eggs, lightly beaten

1 teaspoon crushed red pepper

2 1/2 cups grated Parmesan cheese

1 (10 ounce) package frozen chopped spinach, thawed and drained

2 tablespoons freshly chopped parsley

1 large tomato, chopped (about 1 cup)

2 pounds fresh or frozen shrimp, peeled and deveined

Salt and pepper

Preheat oven to 350°F.

In a large pot over medium heat, boil the pasta in salted water. Cook to just under al dente, drain, and set aside.

In the same large pot over medium heat, melt the butter. Sauté the onions and garlic in the butter until the onions are translucent. Reduce heat to low and add the milk, oregano, cayenne, eggs, and crushed red pepper. Mix well, and add the pasta, stirring until the pasta is well coated. Add 2 cups of the Parmesan cheese, spinach, 1 tablespoon parsley, tomato, and shrimp. Mix well, salt and pepper to taste, and transfer to a greased 2 3/4-quart or 9 × 13-inch baking dish.

Cover with half of the remaining Parmesan cheese and bake, uncovered, for 45 minutes or until the casserole is bubbly and the shrimp is pink and cooked through. Remove and cover with the remaining Parmesan cheese and remaining parsley. Bake an additional 10 minutes.

Let stand 5 to 10 minutes before serving.

Macaroni and Cheese

There are few things in the world I hold in higher regard than macaroni and cheese. That's probably why I've acquired the nickname Thickness over the years, but to me, a life without macaroni and cheese is a life not lived. A side dish or a meal on its own, with meat or without, with eight cheeses or one, macaroni and cheese is always a crowd pleaser.

Rumored to have been created by Thomas Jefferson and made wildly popular by Kraft, macaroni and cheese has become one of the most sought-after American comfort foods. Variations of the dish are now served at some of the top American restaurants in cities all over the country.

There are two schools of thought when it comes to baked macaroni and cheese. For some, macaroni and cheese begins with a white or béchamel sauce to which cheese is added. This makes for a very creamy dish. For others, cheese is the one and only star. These cheesy dishes can be served much like lasagna, because they're firm on the inside and brown on top and around the edges.

I tend to fall into the second category, and probably only because I ate in far too many cafeterias as a child. Seduction (page 152), a take on my signature mac and corn casserole, is held together with five cheeses and only incorporates a little milk to keep it moist, while my Classic Baked Macaroni and Cheese (page 150) incorporates a white sauce, egg, and a tablespoon of Dijon mustard. You'll find a lot of cayenne pepper on these pages—not because I'm trying to catch your mouth on fire, but because I've found that just a hint really brings out the flavor of cheese, especially cheddar.

Whatever kind of baked macaroni and cheese you're seeking, you'll most likely find it here.

Four-Cheese Mac with Peas

FILE UNDER: Oh So Good but Bad for You, Vegetarian

Sneaking peas into a tuna noodle or macaroni casserole was the only way my parents could get me to eat them as a kid. I recently tried that trick on some kids with this recipe, and it still works like a charm. As an adult, I appreciate the pop of the sweet peas in the dish. A variation on this dish includes half a pound of bacon, which is cooked into the casserole. The leftover bacon grease is used to toast the bread crumbs, infusing the bacon flavor throughout.

SERVES 3 TO 4

1 pound medium shell pasta

1 large white onion, diced

2 cloves garlic, minced

1 tablespoon olive oil

3 tablespoons butter

1 1/2 cups milk

1 tablespoon flour

1/4 pound sharp cheddar, shredded or cubed

1/4 pound white cheddar, shredded or cubed

1/4 pound Gruyère, shredded or cubed

1/4 pound Parmesan, grated

1 (16 ounce) bag frozen sweet peas

Salt and pepper

2 to 3 tablespoons bread crumbs

Preheat oven to 400°F.

Parboil the pasta, drain, and set aside.

In a large pot over high heat, sauté the onions and garlic in the olive oil. When the onions begin to brown, reduce heat to low. Add 2 tablespoons of the butter, the milk, and the flour, stirring constantly. When the flour and milk are mixed well, add the sharp cheddar while continuing to stir. When the sharp cheddar begins to melt, add the white cheddar. When the cheeses are melted, add the shells and stir. When the shells are well coated, add the Gruyère and all but a tablespoon of the Parmesan. Mix well and add the peas. Salt and pepper to taste.

When everything is thoroughly mixed, transfer to a buttered 2-quart baking dish.

In a small bowl, mix the remaining Parmesan with the bread crumbs and the remaining table-spoon of butter, softened. Cover the casserole with half of this mixture, saving the other half.

Bake, uncovered, for 35 to 40 minutes or until bubbly. Remove and cover with the remaining topping. Bake for an additional 10 to 15 minutes.

Let stand 10 minutes before serving.

VARIATION: The bread crumbs are sautéed in the leftover bacon grease, then used as a crispy topping so the bacon flavor is apparent throughout. Be sure to blot the bacon with a paper towel to remove the excess grease before chopping it, or you'll end up with an incredibly greasy casserole.

In a skillet over medium heat, cook the bacon until it is almost crispy. Remove the bacon and set aside to cool. Finely chop the bacon and add it to the mixture before it's transferred to the casserole dish. Add the bread crumbs to the bacon grease and sauté for about 1 minute. Remove the bread crumb mixture and set aside to use for the topping.

Eight-Cheese Macaroni

FILE UNDER: Oh So Good but Bad for You, Vegetarian

This solid macaroni dish is made with eight cheeses and falls into the cut-it-with-a-knife macaroni category (a knife I'd like to lick). So if you prefer your macaroni on the creamy side, this dish may not be for you. But for those who love their macaroni and cheese to have some structural integrity, this is the mama of all macaroni and cheese dishes. While I suggest eight cheeses, if you can't find one, or just feel like changing things up, I encourage you to throw in your favorite "wild card cheese."　　　SERVES 5 TO 6

1 pound medium shell pasta

1 large white onion, diced

2 cloves garlic, minced

1 tablespoon olive oil

3 tablespoons butter

$1/4$ cup grated Parmesan

$1/4$ cup grated Romano

$1/4$ cup shredded Gruyère

$1/4$ cup shredded sharp cheddar

$1/4$ cup shredded white cheddar

$1/4$ cup ricotta cheese

$1/4$ pound Pecorino, shredded

$1/4$ pound Gouda, cubed

$1/2$ teaspoon cayenne pepper

$1/2$ cup milk

Salt and pepper

2 to 3 tablespoons bread crumbs

Preheat oven to 350°F.

In a large pot of salted water, cook the pasta to just under al dente. Drain and set aside.

In the same large pot, over high heat, sauté the onions and garlic in the olive oil and 2 tablespoons of the butter. When the onions begin to brown, reduce the heat to low, add the pasta, and mix well. Gradually begin to add all the cheeses (save half of the Parmesan), the cayenne, and the milk, stirring continuously. Salt and pepper to taste.

When everything is thoroughly mixed, transfer to a buttered $2^1/2$ to $2^3/4$-quart baking dish. (You're going to lose a lot of your cheese to the inside of the pot you were mixing in. It's okay, you have some to spare.)

In a small bowl, mix the remaining Parmesan with the bread crumbs and the remaining tablespoon of butter, softened. Cover the casserole with half of this mixture, saving the other half.

Bake, uncovered, for 35 to 40 minutes or until bubbly. Remove and cover with the remaining topping. Bake for an additional 10 to 15 minutes.

Let stand 10 minutes before serving.

Classic Baked Macaroni and Cheese

FILE UNDER: Oh So Good but Bad for You, Vegetarian

For traditionalists, a basic elbow macaroni with a gooey cheese sauce and bread crumbs on top is the way to go. You've probably had some version of this at a diner, potluck, or cafeteria. This one probably has a few more ingredients and is a little more time-consuming, but if there's one thing in the world one should master, it's macaroni and cheese.   SERVE 4 TO 5

1/2 pound elbow macaroni	2 cups milk
3 tablespoons butter	1/4 teaspoon cayenne
1 tablespoon olive oil	1 egg, lightly beaten
1 large white onion, diced	1/4 cup grated Parmesan cheese
2 cloves garlic, minced or pressed	2 cups shredded cheddar cheese
3 tablespoons flour	Salt and pepper
1 tablespoon Dijon mustard or dry mustard	1/4 cup bread crumbs

Preheat oven to 350°F.

Parboil the macaroni, drain, and set aside.

In a large saucepan over medium heat, melt 2 tablespoons of the butter. Add the olive oil, onions, and garlic and sauté until the onions are translucent. Add the flour and mustard, stirring or whisking constantly. Add the milk and cayenne and stir for 3 to 5 minutes. Slowly add the egg while continuing to stir. Add the pasta and mix well. When the pasta is fully coated, add half of the Parmesan and all of the cheddar. Salt and pepper to taste. Mix well. Transfer to a buttered or greased 2 1/2-quart casserole dish.

In a small bowl, mix the bread crumbs with the remaining tablespoon of softened butter and the remaining Parmesan. Evenly distribute half of this mixture on top of the casserole.

Bake, uncovered, for 30 to 35 minutes or until bubbly.

Remove from oven and cover with the remaining bread crumb mix. Bake for an additional 5 to 10 minutes.

Let stand 5 to 10 minutes before serving.

Mac and Cheese with Tuna and Peas

One part trashy, three parts delicious, this macaroni and cheese with (yes, canned) tuna and peas is the perfect comfort food. Maybe not what you'd want to make for a white-napkin dinner party, but perfect for a night in with some Netflix and beer. **SERVES 4 TO 5**

1 pound medium shell pasta

1 large white onion, diced

2 cloves garlic, minced

1 tablespoon olive oil

3 tablespoons butter

1 1/2 cups milk

1 tablespoon flour

1/2 pound sharp cheddar, shredded or cubed

1/2 pound white cheddar, shredded or cubed

1/2 pound Parmesan, grated

2 (6 ounce) cans white albacore tuna, drained

1 (16 ounce) bag frozen sweet peas

Salt and pepper

2 to 3 tablespoons bread crumbs

Preheat oven to 350°F.

Parboil the pasta, drain, and set aside.

In a large pot over high heat, sauté the onions and garlic in the olive oil. When the onions begin to brown, reduce the heat to low, add 2 tablespoons of the butter, the milk, and the flour, stirring continuously. When the flour and milk are mixed well, add the sharp cheddar while continuing to stir. When the sharp cheddar begins to melt, add the white cheddar. When the cheeses are melted, add the shells and stir. When the shells are well coated, add all but 1 tablespoon of the Parmesan. Mix well, then add the tuna and peas and stir. Add salt and pepper to taste.

When everything is thoroughly mixed, transfer to a buttered 2 1/2-quart baking dish.

In a small bowl, mix the remaining Parmesan with the bread crumbs and the remaining tablespoon of butter, softened. Cover the casserole with half of this mixture, saving the other half.

Bake, uncovered, for 35 to 40 minutes or until bubbly. Remove and cover with the remaining topping. Bake for an additional 10 to 15 minutes.

Let stand 10 minutes before serving.

Seduction (Mac and Corn 2.0)

FILE UNDER: **Oh So Good but Bad for You, Vegetarian**

Don't blame me if every person who eats this wants to sleep with you, marry you, or both. Or blame me if you want. There's a reason this, my signature casserole, is called "Seduction." And it's not because the ingredients themselves are sexy. I'll leave the rest to your imagination. This dish is served best with a bottle of dry red, a mixed green salad, and your favorite play list. (You might want to skip the garlic if you're actually trying to seduce someone.)

SERVES 4 TO 6

1 pound cavatelli

2 cloves garlic, minced

1 large white onion, diced

$1/4$ cup olive oil

$1/2$ cup milk

$1/2$ pound sharp cheddar, cubed or shredded

$1/2$ pound white cheddar, cubed or shredded

$1/2$ pound Gruyère, cubed or shredded

$1/2$ cup grated Parmesan

1 (10 ounce) bag Cascadian Farm frozen organic sweet corn

Salt and pepper

$1/2$ pound fresh mozzarella, cubed

2 plum tomatoes, thinly sliced

Preheat oven to 350°F.

Parboil the pasta, drain, and set aside.

In a large pot over medium heat, sauté the garlic and onion in 2 to 3 tablespoons of the olive oil. When the onions begin to brown, reduce the heat to low, add the milk, and stir. Add both of the cheddars and the Gruyère while continuing to stir. When the cheeses begin to melt, add the pasta, ,stirring until the pasta is well coated. Add half of the Parmesan ($1/4$ cup) and stir. Add the corn while continuing to stir (it should go in frozen). Salt and pepper to taste. Add the mozzarella and stir.

When thoroughly mixed, transfer to a $2^3/4$-quart buttered or greased casserole dish and bake, uncovered, for 35 to 40 minutes or until bubbly.

Remove from oven and cover with the sliced tomatoes and the rest of the Parmesan cheese. Bake for about 15 more minutes.

Let stand 10 minutes before eating.

Mac and Corn (1.0)

If Seduction (page 152) is Mac and Corn 2.0, this is Mac and Corn 1.0. Still an upgrade from how I was first introduced to it (Kraft Macaroni and Cheese with a can of creamed corn), it's the first casserole I made for my New York friends. At the party, a restaurateur friend I can only describe as the Ultimate Food Snob devoured three servings, then gave up on plates altogether and ate straight from the dish with a plastic spoon. With this recipe, we're really going for gooey on the inside, crusty on top. But use quality cheeses, or you're going to end up with a plastic-y casserole.

OPTIONAL: You can add as many cheeses as your little heart desires. The more the merrier, but if you're using more than four, keep them to ¼ cup per cheese.   SERVES 6

1 pound small shell or elbow macaroni

½ stick butter

1 cup milk

4 cups (1 pound) shredded cheddar cheese

½ cup shredded Monterey Jack cheese

1 cup finely grated Parmesan cheese

Salt and pepper

1 (16 ounce) bag frozen whole-kernel sweet corn

Preheat oven to 350°F.

Parboil the pasta, drain, and set aside.

In a large pot over medium heat, mix the butter, milk, and 1 cup of the cheddar cheese. Stir until smooth. Add the pasta and mix until well coated. Gradually add 2 cups of the cheddar cheese to the mixture, stirring constantly. Once mixed and the cheddar begins to melt, add the Monterey Jack to the mixture and stir. Add ¼ cup of the Parmesan cheese and continue to stir. Salt and pepper to taste. Gradually add the corn while continuing to stir.

When thoroughly mixed, transfer to a buttered 2½-quart casserole dish. Sprinkle ½ cup of the cheddar and 1 tablespoon of the Parmesan on top. Bake, uncovered, for 35 to 45 minutes or until bubbly and lightly browned.

Remove from oven and layer remainder of the Parmesan and cheddar on top. Bake 5 to 10 more minutes or until top layer is lightly browned.

Let stand 5 minutes before serving.

Cheese Love

FILE UNDER: Oh So Good but Bad for You, Vegetarian

This recipe won first place at my Third Annual Casserole Party in 2007, and as one judge noted, it was "most worth the heart attack it might give you." The dish's creators, Zachary Schulman and Graham Kelly, claim the secret is in the brand of cheese they used, mostly available in the New York area and online at www.cowsoutside.com, but of course, any quality cheddar will do. But buyer beware: if you use the cheap stuff, you won't experience the depth of true cheese love.   SERVES 5 TO 6

1 pound shiitake mushrooms, stems removed, caps quartered

10 to 11 tablespoons butter

1 pound rotini or gemelli pasta

1 bunch kale, stems removed

4 cups whole milk

20 ounces shredded Bobolink Cave-Ripened Cheddar or other cheddar cheese

10 ounces smoked Gouda, rind removed, shredded

6 tablespoons flour

3/4 teaspoon paprika

Salt and freshly ground pepper to taste

Preheat oven to 350°F.

Sauté the mushrooms in 6 to 7 tablespoons of the butter over medium heat until they reduce significantly in volume. Continue cooking until they become golden brown. Turn down the heat and cook until the mushrooms reduce further and become a darker brown. Remove from heat.

Cook the pasta in boiling water a few minutes less than al dente. Drain and rinse under cold water. Blanch and shock the kale. Drain the water from the leaves and chop. Heat the milk to a simmer in a large pot. Toss the shredded cheeses together in a bowl.

Melt the remaining 4 tablespoons of butter in a large heavy saucepan. Add the flour and whisk over low heat for about 5 minutes. Try not to let the flour and butter mixture brown. Remove from heat.

Add the hot milk to the flour mixture and whisk well. Add the paprika, season with salt and pepper, and return to medium heat, whisking constantly until the mixture thickens, about 5 minutes. Begin to mix in the cheese one handful at a time. Add about ⅔ of the cheese to this mix, reserving about ⅓ of the cheese. Toss the pasta, kale, and mushrooms into the mix and stir to incorporate. Taste and adjust seasonings. Remove from heat.

Transfer the mixture to a buttered 9×13-inch casserole dish. Evenly top with the remaining cheese. Sprinkle with pepper.

Bake until hot and a little bubbly, about 20 to 25 minutes.

Turn on the broiler and broil for about 3 to 5 minutes until the top becomes sizzling hot and deep golden brown color.

Mac and Corn Light (0.5)

FILE UNDER: Not So Bad for You, Vegetarian

While this is by no means as decadent or delicious as any of the other mac and cheese dishes in this book, it's a quick fix when you're craving something warm and gooey, and it's not even that bad for you. Not that it's great for you, either. This dish calls for creamed corn (which, by the way, only means that the corn has been creamed—it doesn't contain cream), which provides the moisture you'd get from the milk and butter in the not-so-healthy versions of this dish (see Mac and Corn 1.0 and Seduction). This can be spruced up with some sautéed onion and garlic, but that takes away the whole "quick fix" thing.   SERVES 4

1 box shells and cheddar (I prefer Annie's)

1 box shells and white cheddar (I prefer Annie's)

1 (10.5 ounce) can creamed corn

Salt and pepper

10 to 12 ounces sweet whole-kernel corn (frozen or canned), drained

$1/4$ cup low-fat cheddar cheese, shredded, optional

Preheat oven to 350°F.

Parboil the shells from both boxes (this will take no time, so watch them carefully). Drain and set aside.

In the same pot, mix the contents of the powdered cheese packets with the can of creamed corn. Stir until you can't tell that the cheese was once a powder (I know powdered cheese sounds gross, but it will be good, I promise). Add the shells and stir until they are coated with sauce. Salt and pepper to taste (I'm not going to lie, you need a lot of pepper). Gradually add the whole-kernel corn while continuing to stir.

Transfer the mixture to a 2 or $2^1/2$-quart casserole dish.

Bake for 35 to 45 minutes or until lightly browned on top.

OPTIONAL: Remove and sprinkle shredded low-fat cheddar cheese on top, then bake 5 to 10 more minutes or until top layer is lightly browned.

Mac and Cheese with Hot Dogs

FILE UNDER: Oh So Good but Bad for You

When I was little, my grandma Ruth would make Kraft Macaroni and Cheese with cut-up hot dogs every time we'd visit. She'd give it a good dose of pepper and serve it to us with ginger ale in miniature crystal goblets. Even now, as an adult, it continues to be one of my favorite dishes. I just have it with a bigger glass filled with wine, not ginger ale. While I'm not necessarily recommending you use Kraft Macaroni and Cheese out of a box (I'll do that on my own when no one is watching), if you wanted to, you'd certainly save yourself some trouble and I wouldn't tell. If you don't want to, this recipe will do just fine.   SERVES 5 TO 6

1 pound medium elbow macaroni

1/2 large white onion, diced

1 tablespoon olive oil

1 1/2 cups milk

1 tablespoon flour

1/2 pound sharp cheddar, shredded or cubed

1/2 pound white chedddar, shredded or cubed

6 all-beef hot dogs, cut into 1/2-inch pieces

Salt and pepper

4 tablespoons bread crumbs

Preheat oven to 350°F.

Parboil the pasta, drain, and set aside.

In a large pot over high heat, sauté the onions in the olive oil. When the onions begin to brown, reduce the heat to low. Add the milk and flour, stirring constantly. When the flour and milk are mixed well, add the sharp cheddar while continuing to stir. When the sharp cheddar begins to melt, add the white cheddar. When the cheeses are melted, add the macaroni and stir. When the macaroni is well coated, add the hot dogs and mix well. Salt and pepper to taste.

Transfer to a buttered 2 1/2 to 2 3/4-quart greased or buttered baking dish.

Bake, uncovered, for 35 to 40 minutes or until bubbly and golden on top. Remove and cover with the bread crumbs. Bake for an additional 10 minutes.

Let stand 10 minutes before serving.

Chorizo Mac

FILE UNDER: Oh So Good but Bad for You

This is like mac and cheese with hot dogs, but for adults. The garlic and chorizo add a ton of flavor. I like to use a really spicy chorizo, but the level of heat is up to you. The bread crumbs are mixed with butter and put on top to give the casserole a crispy topping, and they counteract the heat of the chorizo if you choose to use a spicy one.   SERVES 4 TO 5

1 pound medium elbow macaroni

1 large white onion, diced

2 gloves garlic, minced or diced

1 tablespoon olive oil

2 cups milk

1 tablespoon flour

1/2 pound white cheddar, shredded or cubed

1/2 pound Parmesan cheese, shredded or grated

1 pound cured chorizo, cut into 1/2-inch pieces

Salt and pepper

4 tablespoons bread crumbs

1 tablespoon butter, softened

Preheat oven to 350°F.

In a large pot of boiling water, parboil the macaroni, drain, and set aside.

In a large pot over high heat, sauté the onions and garlic in the olive oil. When the onions begin to brown, reduce the heat to low. Add the milk and flour, stirring constantly. When the flour and milk are mixed well, add the cheddar while continuing to stir. When the cheddar beings to melt, add the Parmesan and mix well. When the cheeses are melted, add the macaroni and stir until well coated. Add the chorizo, salt and pepper to taste, and mix well.

Transfer to a buttered 2 1/2 to 2 3/4-quart greased or buttered baking dish.

In a small bowl, mix the butter and bread crumbs. Put half of this mixture on top of the casserole, distributing evenly.

Bake, uncovered, for 35 to 40 minutes or until bubbly and golden on top. Remove and cover with the remaining bread crumb mixture and bake for an additional 10 minutes.

Let stand 10 minutes before serving.

This incredibly rich macaroni and cheese incorporates broccoli and mushrooms to balance out the richness of the cheeses. Smoked Gouda can be used in place of the Gruyère, or just added for extra cheesiness. While this certainly isn't a healthy dinner, it's a delicious way to eat your green veggies. This recipe calls for ½ teaspoon of cayenne pepper to enhance the flavor of the cheeses, but feel free to leave it out if you don't like the heat.   SERVES 6 TO 7

1 pound cavatelli

2 large white onions, chopped

2 to 3 tablespoons olive oil

3 cloves garlic, minced

2 cups baby portobello mushrooms, chopped

2 tablespoons butter

1 tablespoon flour

1 cup milk

½ teaspoon cayenne pepper

½ pound sharp cheddar cheese, cubed

1 cup Parmesan cheese, grated

3 cups broccoli florets, lightly steamed

¼ pound Gruyère, cubed

Salt and pepper

Preheat oven to 375°F.

In a large pot, boil the cavatelli to just under al dente. Drain and set aside.

In a skillet over medium heat, sauté the onions in the olive oil until the onions become translucent. Add the garlic and mushrooms and sauté for another 3 to 5 minutes, stirring occasionally. Set aside.

In the bottom of the same large pot in which you cooked your pasta (a nonstick pot is best, but not necessary), melt the butter over medium heat and add the flour. When the two are combined, add the milk, cayenne, cheddar, and half of the Parmesan. When the cheeses begin to melt, add the onion mixture and the broccoli, then mix well. Slowly add the pasta, mixing until all of the noodles are coated. Add the Gruyère, salt and pepper to taste, and transfer to a greased or buttered 9×13-inch baking dish.

Sprinkle with the remaining Parmesan and bake, uncovered, for 45 minutes or until bubbly and brown around the edges.

Let stand 10 minutes before serving.

Brooklyn Label's Basil Mac Casserole

FILE UNDER: Oh So Good but Bad for You, Vegetarian

This casserole, courtesy of Cody Utzman, co-owner and chef of Brooklyn Label in Greenpoint, Brooklyn, is the kind of dish you would refer to as "ridiculous" if you weren't so busy shoving the next bite into your mouth. Made in three steps (béchamel sauce, pesto sauce, and pasta), the recipe feeds ten to twelve, and you should most definitely make it for your next dinner party. This calls for a large shell pasta, and while any old kind will do, Cody recommends Bionaturae Organic Drum Semolina Chiocciole.

SERVES 10 TO 12

2 pounds large shell pasta

4 heirloom tomatoes, coarsely chopped

Pesto

4 cloves garlic

2 bunches fresh basil

1 cup olive oil

1 cup toasted walnuts

Juice of 1 lemon

$^1/_2$ cup grated Parmesan

Cheese Sauce

2 white onions, diced

4 cloves garlic, minced

$^1/_2$ cup olive oil

1 stick butter

1 cup flour

$^1/_2$ gallon whole milk

1 pound Gruyère, grated

2 cups grated Parmesan

1 teaspoon fresh clove

$^1/_2$ teaspoon nutmeg

Salt and pepper

Parboil the pasta, drain, and set aside.

Combine pesto ingredients in a food processor, and set aside.

Preheat oven to 350°F.

In a large pan over medium heat, sauté the onion and garlic in the olive oil and butter until the onions are translucent. Add the flour and stir constantly until the flour is completely integrated into the olive oil and butter. Add the milk and whisk constantly until the mixture is thick. Add the Gruyère and Parmesan, stirring constantly until the cheese is melted. Add the clove and nutmeg, and salt and pepper to taste.

In a large bowl, mix the pasta, cheese sauce, and pesto (reserving some pesto for topping). Transfer to a 5-quart baking dish (or two smaller dishes). Bake, uncovered, for 40 to 45 minutes until bubbly and golden on top.

Serve with a drizzle of pesto and fresh tomatoes on top.

Macaroni with Peas, Carrots, and Onions

FILE UNDER: Oh So Good but Bad for You, Vegetarian

This macaroni and cheese with peas, carrots, and onions may sound like it belongs on a plastic lunch tray, but when the carrots and onions are sautéed together with garlic, it's really a savory dinner. I had this quite often as a child, and still like to eat it as an adult. I feel like I'm getting a few nutrients mixed in with my pasta and cheese, and the carrots and peas are an unexpected, yet totally fitting, surprise.

SERVES 4 TO 5

1 pound medium elbow macaroni

1 large white onion, diced

3 cloves garlic, minced or pressed

1 cup chopped raw carrot

3 tablespoons olive oil

2 cups milk

1 tablespoon flour

1/2 pound sharp cheddar, shredded or cubed

1/2 pound Parmesan cheese, shredded or grated

1 (16 ounce) bag frozen sweet peas

Salt and pepper

1 tablespoon butter, softened

4 tablespoons bread crumbs

Preheat oven to 350°F.

Parboil the pasta, drain, and set aside.

In a large pot over high heat, sauté the onions, garlic, and carrots in the olive oil. When the onions begin to brown and the carrots become soft, reduce the heat to low. Add the milk and flour, stirring constantly. When the flour and milk are mixed well, add the cheddar while continuing to stir. When the cheddar begins to melt, add the Parmesan and mix well. When the cheeses are melted, add the macaroni and stir to coat. Add the peas and mix well. Salt and pepper to taste.

Transfer to a buttered 2 1/2-quart greased or buttered baking dish.

In a small bowl, mix the butter and bread crumbs. Put half of this mixture on top of the casserole, distributing evenly.

Bake, uncovered, for 35 to 40 minutes or until bubbly and golden on top. Remove from oven and cover with the remaining bread crumb mixture. Bake for an additional 10 minutes.

Let stand 10 minutes before serving.

Creamy, Cheesy Penne

FILE UNDER: Oh So Good but Bad for You, Vegetarian

With less bite than a pure cheddar-based macaroni, this creamy penne dish is still savory and ridiculously decadent. The cheddar, ricotta, and Parmesan work well together, and the combination works even better when mixed with sour cream.

VARIATION: You can add 8 to 16 ounces of frozen sweet peas, which can and should go in the mix right before you transfer it to the baking dish. SERVES 6

1 pound penne pasta	4 ounces sour cream
1 large white onion, chopped	1/2 cup grated Parmesan cheese
2 tablespoons olive oil	1/2 cup shredded sharp cheddar cheese
2 tablespoons butter, softened	Salt and pepper
1/2 cup milk	1/4 cup bread crumbs
4 ounces ricotta cheese	1 tablespoon chopped fresh parsley

Preheat oven to 350°F.

Parboil the pasta, drain, and set aside.

In a large saucepan over medium heat, sauté the onion in the olive oil and 1 tablespoon of the butter until the onions are translucent. Reduce the heat to low and add the milk, ricotta, sour cream, and half of the Parmesan and stir. When fully mixed, add the pasta and stir. When the pasta is fully coated, add the cheddar cheese and mix well. Salt and pepper to taste.

Transfer to a 2½-quart buttered baking dish.

In a small bowl, mix together the bread crumbs, remaining Parmesan, and 1 tablespoon of the butter. Sprinkle half of the topping over the macaroni mixture. Add parsley to the remaining mixture.

Bake, uncovered, 30 to 35 minutes, or until the top is golden.

Remove from oven and sprinkle the remaining mixture on top and bake an additional 10 minutes.

Let stand 5 to 10 minutes before serving.

Spicy Mac

Even though I'm not a huge fan of jalapeños, they work really well in this dish. I've called for two here, but I like my spicy food to be spicy. It is called Spicy Mac, after all. If you like just a little heat, use one and cut the cayenne. But remember, the cayenne really enhances the flavor of the cheddar cheese.

SERVES 4 TO 6

1 pound bow-tie pasta

1 large white onion, chopped

2 cloves garlic, minced

2 jalapeños, seeded and minced

4 tablespoons butter

1 tablespoon olive oil

1 tablespoon flour

2 cups milk

1 (28 ounce) can pureed tomatoes

$\frac{1}{2}$ teaspoon cayenne pepper, or to taste

Salt and pepper

1 cup shredded Monterey Jack cheese

1 cup shredded sharp cheddar

1 cup grated Parmesan

Preheat oven to 350°F.

In a large pot of boiling water, parboil the pasta. Drain and set aside.

In a large pan over medium heat, sauté the onion, garlic, and jalapeño in the butter and olive oil. When the onion becomes translucent, add the flour and stir continuously for about 1 minute, then add the milk and stir. Add the pureed tomatoes and cayenne and mix well. Salt and pepper to taste. Add the pasta and mix well. When the pasta is coated, add the Monterey Jack and cheddar cheeses and half of the Parmesan.

Transfer the mixture to a 2¾-quart baking dish and bake, uncovered, 25 to 35 minutes or until bubbly.

Remove from the oven, cover with the remaining Parmesan, and bake approximately 10 more minutes.

Let stand 10 minutes before serving.

Parmesan and Mushroom Mac

There are few combinations I love more than mushrooms, cheese, and onions. But throw in bow-tie pasta and bread crumbs, and I could live off this dish for the rest of my life. There's only one thing that could make this more decadent, and that's bacon. But I'm not trying to give you a heart attack. If I were, I'd tell you to add a half cup to a cup of chopped, freshly cooked bacon.

SERVES 4

$^1/_2$ pound bow-tie pasta

1 large white onion, diced

2 tablespoons olive oil

2 tablespoons butter

$1^1/_2$ cups baby portobello mushrooms, cleaned and sliced

1 tablespoon flour

2 cups milk

Salt and pepper

$2^1/_2$ cups Parmesan cheese

$^1/_4$ cup bread crumbs

1 teaspoon chopped fresh parsley

Preheat oven to 350°F.

Parboil the pasta, drain, and set aside.

In a large pan over medium heat, sauté the onion in the olive oil and 1 tablespoon of the butter until the onions are translucent. Add the mushrooms and sauté, stirring occasionally, for about 2 minutes. Add the flour and stir quickly, then slowly add the milk while continuing to stir. Salt and pepper to taste, and let simmer for about 3 to 4 minutes, stirring occasionally. Add $2^1/_4$ cups of the Parmesan cheese and mix well.

If there's room in your pan (or in a large bowl), mix the pasta and the sauce, ensuring that the pasta is fully coated. Salt and pepper to taste (again). Transfer to a greased or buttered 2-quart baking dish.

In a small bowl, mix the remaining tablespoon of butter (softened) with the bread crumbs and parsley. Evenly distribute half of this mixture over the casserole.

Bake, uncovered, for 30 to 35 minutes or until bubbly.

Remove from the oven and cover with the remaining bread crumb mixture. Bake approximately 10 more minutes.

Let stand 5 to 10 minutes before serving.

Macaroni with Goat Cheese and Sweet Peas

FILE UNDER: Oh So Good but Bad for You

Goat cheese doesn't melt like regular cheese, so this macaroni with goat cheese and sweet peas also has some help from the ever-friendly Parmesan. And the cheese sauce is based on a roux, a mixture of flour and butter, with the Parmesan and goat cheese incorporated to create one fairly creamy sauce. Also, I love goat cheese with anything green, hence the peas.

A variation on this dish calls for a half pound of bacon. Instructions, which differ slightly from the original recipe, follow.

SERVES 6

1 pound bow-tie pasta	2 cups milk
1 large white onion, finely chopped	1/4 teaspoon cayenne pepper
2 cloves garlic, minced or diced	Salt and pepper to taste
3 tablespoons olive oil	6 ounces goat cheese, crumbled
2 tablespoons butter	1/2 cup grated Parmesan cheese
2 tablespoons flour	1 (16 ounce) bag frozen sweet peas

Preheat oven to 350°F.

Parboil the pasta, drain, and set aside.

In a large saucepan over medium heat, sauté the onions and garlic in the olive oil until the onions are translucent. Add the butter to the saucepan, and when the butter is melted, add the flour and mix quickly and thoroughly. When the butter and flour are mixed, add the milk and stir continuously until the mixture thickens. Add the cayenne, salt, and pepper. Mix well, then slowly add the goat cheese while continuing to stir. When the goat cheese is integrated, add the Parmesan cheese and continue to stir. Reduce the heat to low and let simmer for about 3 minutes, stirring occasionally. Add the peas and mix well.

Transfer the pasta to a buttered or greased 2-quart or larger baking dish. Pour the cheese sauce over the pasta.

Bake, uncovered, 25 to 35 minutes or until bubbly.

Let stand 5 to 10 minutes before serving.

VARIATION: The bread crumbs are sautéed in the leftover bacon grease then used as a crispy topping, giving the casserole a bacon flavor. Be sure to blot the bacon with a paper towel to remove the excess grease before chopping it, or you'll end up with an incredibly greasy casserole.

In a skillet over medium heat, cook the bacon until it is almost crispy. Remove the bacon and set aside to cool. Finely chop the bacon and add it to the mixture before it's transferred to the casserole dish. Add the bread crumbs to the bacon grease and sauté for about 1 minute. Remove the bread crumb mixture and set aside to use for the topping.

Let's Pretend It's Healthy Mac and Cheese

FILE UNDER: **Not So Bad for You, Vegetarian**

While this isn't the most healthy dish in the world, it's healthier than most of the macaroni and cheese dishes in this book because it incorporates more mushrooms and uses a tricolor Rotini and skim milk. So if you're looking to indulge just a little, try this rotini mac. While it won't be dripping with cheese, the cayenne will enhance the flavor of the cheddar that's in this dish.

SERVES 4

½ pound tricolor rotini

1 large onion, finely chopped

3 cloves garlic, minced

3 tablespoons olive oil

½ cup cleaned and chopped baby portobello mushrooms

2 tablespoons butter

1 tablespoon flour

2 cups skim milk

1 teaspoon Dijon mustard

¼ teaspoon cayenne pepper

1 cup grated cheddar cheese

Preheat oven to 350°F.

Parboil the pasta, drain, and set aside.

In a large pan over medium heat, sauté the onion and garlic in the olive oil until the onions are translucent. Add the mushrooms and sauté for 1 to 2 minutes, then add the butter. When the butter is melted, add the flour, stirring quickly and constantly. When the butter and flour are fully integrated, add the milk. Stir until the mixture begins to thicken. Add the mustard and cayenne, then slowly add the cheddar cheese while stirring.

Add the cooked rotini to a lightly greased 2-quart baking dish. Pour the cheese mixture over the pasta and bake, uncovered, for 25 to 30 minutes or until bubbly.

Let stand 5 minutes before serving.

It took me a few years to really appreciate the taste of garlic as anything more than an accent. But now that I do, I sometimes like to feature it prominently in a dish, like I do in this garlic mac. My Italian friends love it, but then again they love anything with garlic. If you do, too, this dish is the perfect way to serve up macaroni and cheese with a twist.   SERVES 4 TO 5

4 tablespoons olive oil

Salt

2 cloves garlic, minced or pressed

1 pound elbow macaroni

2 tablespoons butter

10 cloves garlic, sliced

1 large white onion, finely chopped

1 cup milk

1 cup shredded sharp cheddar cheese

1 cup shredded white cheddar cheese

1 cup grated Parmesan cheese

Pepper

$1/2$ teaspoon cayenne pepper, or to taste

Preheat oven to 350°F.

Bring a large pot of water to a boil with 2 tablespoons of the olive oil, a teaspoon of salt, and the 2 minced or pressed garlic cloves. Parboil the macaroni in this mixture, drain, and set aside.

In the same large pot, over medium heat, melt the 2 tablespoons of butter and sauté half of the sliced garlic in the butter for about 2 minutes. Add the remaining olive oil and the onions. Sauté the onions until they begin to brown around the edges, stirring frequently. Reduce the heat to low and slowly add the milk while stirring. When the milk becomes hot, add the pasta and stir. When the pasta is fully coated, slowly add both cheddars and half of the Parmesan while continuing to stir. When everything is well mixed, add the remainder of the garlic, then add salt, pepper, and cayenne to taste.

Transfer the mixture to a buttered or greased 2-quart or larger baking dish. Cover with half of the remaining Parmesan and bake for about 25 minutes or until bubbly.

Remove from oven and cover with the remaining Parmesan and bake for an additional 10 minutes.

Let stand 5 to 10 minutes before serving.

I know. I just turned the world, as you know it, upside down. This book is subtitled *Hot Stuff for Your Oven*, and I'm giving you stove-top recipes.

In the midst of writing this book, I discovered some amazing one-dish recipes that just don't need to be baked. Sometimes it was by accident and other times I was cooking in a kitchen with very little ventilation in the middle of August and needed to find a way to get the cooking done as quickly as possible. Plus, the stove is pretty damn close to the oven, is it not?

In this chapter you'll find an easy paella from Chef Alex Ureña (who knew paella could be easy?), a one-pot jerk chicken and rice dish from the best Caribbean chef I know, and my mom's "lazy woman's cabbage roll," which is not a roll at all, so I call it CabbageRole.

Any of these dishes can be transferred to your best vintage Pyrex if you're feeling a little nostalgic for previous chapters, but if you're anything like me, you'll be eating from the pot before you even turn off the flame.

One-Pot Jerk Chicken and Rice

FILE UNDER: **Not So Bad for You, Lactose-Free**

I met Dudanna Watt in the summer of 2007. We were working at a summer camp in New Hampshire. She was in the kitchen, I was in a bunk. No campers in the history of the world have ever eaten so well. I was always amazed at the meals she could create with so few and basic ingredients. Her One-Pot Jerk Chicken and Rice recipe is no exception. How the camp got her, I'll never know. She's a private chef in Bel Air and has cooked her famous Caribbean cuisine for the Red Hot Chili Peppers, 311, Nine Inch Nails, Gwen Stefani, Maroon 5, Incubus, and countless other hungry bands.

While this recipe is prepared entirely on the stove top and is best served fresh, it can be made ahead of time, transferred to a 3-quart casserole dish, refrigerated, and rewarmed in a 350°F oven for 35 to 40 minutes. Just be sure to let it stand a bit after removing it from the fridge and to add some extra broth if you're going to rewarm it.   SERVES 4 TO 5

1 large, whole chicken, cut into at least 8 pieces, or 3 pounds boneless, skinless chicken breasts

1 tablespoon jarred jerk seasoning marinade, or more to taste

1/4 cup vegetable oil

1 yellow onion, thinly sliced

1 sprig fresh thyme leaves, chopped

2 plum tomatoes, diced

3 1/2 to 4 cups chicken stock

1 1/2 cups long-grain parboiled rice

Salt and pepper

Scotch bonnet chile, whole, optional

Rinse the chicken pieces and pat dry with paper towels. Place the chicken in a large bowl, rub with the jerk seasoning and 2 tablespoons of the oil, and cover and marinate for about 30 minutes.

In a large skillet, heat the rest of the oil and sear the chicken on both sides until golden. Set aside.

In the same skillet, add the onion and thyme and sauté until tender, then add the diced tomatoes, stock, and rice. Salt and pepper to taste and mix well.

Place the seared chicken pieces on top of the rice mixture and bring to a boil.

Reduce heat and simmer, covered, until the rice is cooked and the chicken is tender, about 25 minutes. For extra spice, toss in the whole Scotch bonnet chile.

Garnish with sprigs of fresh thyme.

Fresh Kale and Whole Wheat Pasta Sauté

FILE UNDER: Not So Bad for You, Lactose-Free, Vegan, Vegetarian

In what was probably a freak accident of global warming, some fresh kale had popped up in upstate New York in the middle of January and appeared at my local greenmarket. I was so excited by how fresh and green and bountiful it was, I bought a few bunches and rushed right home—only to find I didn't have much to cook it with. What followed was an amazing vegan stove-top dish that I loved so much I made every night, consecutively, until I ran out of the kale.

This can be made in one or two pots, depending on how many dishes you want to do. Here I show you how to make it with one, but I often have pasta boiling in one with my kale sautéing in the other. This recipe can easily be halved or quartered, depending on how many hungry vegans you're feeding. But beware: even the most carnivorous of your dinner guests will eat this up. While it can be made with any kind of pasta, I prefer the Barilla Plus elbows. Larger noodles will overpower the kale, so stick with smaller ones. SERVES 6

1 pound whole wheat elbow pasta

1 large white onion, chopped

2 to 3 cloves garlic, coarsely chopped

1/2 cup olive oil

1 bunch fresh kale, stems removed, torn into 1 to 2-inch pieces

1 to 2 cups water

Sea salt

Freshly ground pepper

In a large pot, boil the pasta to al dente, drain and set aside.

In the same large pot, over medium heat, sauté the onions and garlic in a few tablespoons of the olive oil. When the onions begin to brown around the edges, add the kale and stir. After a few minutes on the heat, the kale will turn a deep green. At this point, pour about 1/2 cup of water over the kale (be careful not to burn yourself!) and stir. Let the kale cook a little longer and repeat the water step a few times until the kale is cooked through and wilted. Add a few pinches of sea salt and some freshly ground pepper to taste.

Add the cooked pasta to the pot and a drizzle or two of the olive oil. Stir. Add more sea salt and freshly ground pepper to taste. Stir again and serve.

Alex Ureña's Easy Paella

FILE UNDER: Not So Bad For You, Gluten-Free (if you use gluten-free stock), Lactose-Free

Alex Ureña, chef and owner of Pamplona restaurant, is known for his modern Spanish cuisine. This paella—a rice dish from Spain—which can sometimes be tricky and complicated, is quite simple and makes for a wonderfully savory and filling dinner for two. It is believed that paella was created by servants mixing the leftovers from royal banquets to take home and feed their families, because it's full of such a wonderful mix of red meat, poultry, and seafood.

SERVES 2

½ onion, cut into small dice

1 red pepper, cut into small dice

3 cloves of garlic, brunoise

1½ tablespoons paprika

4 tablespoons olive oil

1 chicken leg, cut into small pieces

5 ounces rib eye steak, cut into ½-inch pieces

1 fresh link chorizo, sliced

¾ quart chicken stock

½ pound uncooked white rice

3 grams saffron

10 mussels

10 cockles

¼ cup white wine

6 shrimp

Salt and pepper

In a large pan over medium heat, make a sofrito, a well-cooked and fragrant Spanish sauce, by first sautéing the onions, peppers, garlic, and paprika in the olive oil. When the onions begin to brown around the edges, add the chicken, steak, and chorizo. When the meats begin to brown, add the chicken stock and stir. After the meats are fully coated in the sauce, add the rice and saffron and stir.

In a separate pot, over medium heat, cook the mussels and cockles in the white wine until just open. Drain liquid and add it to the rice.

When the rice is almost cooked, add the shrimp and stir. Remove the cockles and mussels from their shells and add to the rice. Salt and pepper to taste. Serve.

Black Beans and Rice

FILE UNDER: Not So Bad for You, Lactose-Free, Vegan, Vegetarian

This recipe, courtesy of my friend Liz Nebiolo, is a simple way to make black beans and rice. While she was taught to use a sofrito—a basic onion or garlic sauce used in Spanish cooking—like me, she prefers to use as few ingredients and steps as possible, and believes that when it comes to food, less is more. So this Italian take on the dish is super-easy to make and is, as Liz says, "Bangin'!"   SERVES 5 TO 6 WITH RICE

½ large Spanish onion, chopped

3 cloves garlic, sliced

½ jalapeño pepper, seeded and chopped

3 tablespoons olive oil

14 ounces crushed tomatoes (about half a large can)

2 (15 ounce) cans black and/or red beans, drained and rinsed

2 bay leaves

½ cup chopped fresh cilantro

Salt and pepper

3 cups cooked white rice

In a medium pan over medium heat, sauté the onion, garlic, and jalapeño in the olive oil. When the onion becomes translucent, add the tomatoes, beans, and bay leaves. Reduce the heat to low and simmer for 30 minutes, stirring occasionally. After 30 minutes, put half of the mixture into a large mixing bowl and mash well with a potato masher. Return the mashed beans to the pot, mix well, and cook for an additional 10 minutes over low heat.

When the mixture is heated through, remove from the heat and remove the bay leaves. Add the cilantro, and salt and pepper to taste. Mix in the rice, salt and pepper again as needed, and serve.

Curry Rice

FILE UNDER: **Not So Bad for You, Lactose-Free, Vegan, Vegetarian**

Another recipe from Liz Nebiolo, this curry rice is made with brown rice and coconut milk, so it's vegan. While this dish has quite a few ingredients, it's easy to make and doesn't need much time on the stove, like most rice-based dishes. If you like the curry taste but not the spice, omit the jalapeño. **SERVES 4**

$1/4$ cup chopped scallions	2 teaspoons paprika
3 cloves garlic, sliced	1 teaspoon saffron
$1/4$ cup carrot, diced small	$1/2$ cup seedless raisins
$1/2$ jalapeño pepper, seeded and chopped	3 to 4 tablespoons curry powder
2 tablespoons olive oil	3 bay leaves
2 cups brown rice	8 cloves
3 cups water	Salt and pepper
6 to 7 ounces coconut milk	

In a medium to large saucepan over medium heat, sauté the scallions, garlic, carrot, and jalapeño in the olive oil. After 2 to 3 minutes, add the rice, water, coconut milk, paprika, saffron, raisins, and curry powder.

Wrap the bay leaves and cloves in cheesecloth and submerge them in the rice. Mix well and reduce heat to low.

Cover and let simmer for 15 to 20 minutes or until the rice is cooked through, stirring occasionally.

Remove the cheesecloth and its contents and discard, salt and pepper to taste, and serve.

Lamb and Brown Rice

FILE UNDER: **Not So Bad for You, Gluten-Free (if using gluten-free broth), Lactose-Free**

This simple, high-protein meal combines lamb marinated in a sweet, yet tangy sauce and brown rice with onions and mushrooms. Once the preparation is done, this dish spends a lot of time on the stove while you don't. Because it comes out very brown (lamb, mushrooms, brown rice), pour yourself a glass of red wine and prepare a nice green salad to brighten up the table. SERVES 4 TO 5

2 pounds boneless lean lamb

5 tablespoons olive oil

¼ cup lemon juice

1 teaspoon oregano

3 tablespoons brown sugar

Salt and pepper to taste

1 large white onion, finely chopped

2 cloves garlic, minced or pressed

2 cups baby portobello mushrooms, cleaned and sliced

1 cup uncooked brown rice

2 cups chicken broth

Remove excess fat from the lamb and cut the meat into ½-inch cubes.

In a mixing bowl, combine 2 tablespoons of the olive oil, the lemon juice, oregano, brown sugar, salt, and pepper. Add the lamb cubes, mix well, cover, and refrigerate for at least 1 hour.

After an hour or more, in a large saucepan over medium heat, sauté the onions and garlic in the remaining olive oil until the onions are translucent. Add the lamb and mushrooms and sauté for about 8 minutes. Remove the lamb with a slotted spoon and set aside.

Add to the saucepan the rice and chicken broth. Mix well and when it comes to a boil, reduce the heat to low, replace the lamb, cover, and let simmer for about 1 hour and 15 minutes, or until the lamb and rice are tender, stirring occasionally. Salt and pepper to taste.

Spaghetti Everything

FILE UNDER: Not So Bad for You, Lactose-Free, Vegan, Vegetarian

This super-simple vegan recipe is fresh and savory and will satiate even your hungriest carnivore friend. At least until he goes out for a hamburger at 2 a.m. While the recipe calls for tomatoes and garlic, depending on what I have in the refrigerator, I like to throw in more vegetables that complement the flavors in the dish, like fresh broccoli, cauliflower, and squash or zucchini.

SERVES 5 TO 6

1 pound spaghetti or linguini noodles, broken in half

8 cloves garlic, peeled and sliced

$1/2$ large white onion, finely chopped

5 tablespoons olive oil

1 teaspoon crushed red pepper

Freshly grated pepper

1 cup cherry or grape tomatoes, halved

$1/4$ cup fresh basil, chopped

Sea salt

Parboil pasta in a large pot of salted water. Remove just before al dente, drain, and set aside.

In the bottom of the same pot, over low heat, sauté the garlic and onion in half of the olive oil. After about 2 minutes, add the remaining olive oil, crushed red pepper, and about $1/4$ teaspoon freshly grated pepper. Mix well with a wooden spoon, then add the tomatoes. (If adding additional vegetables, add them now and sauté for 3 to 5 minutes before adding the pasta.) After about 1 minute, add the cooked spaghetti and basil and stir for 1 to 2 minutes over low heat.

Serve directly from pot with a pinch of sea salt if desired.

My mom loves cabbage rolls but doesn't like the work involved in ensuring the structural integrity of each roll, so she started making this "lazy woman's cabbage roll" on the stove top. She, of course, was the lazy woman in question, but was being too hard on herself for creating an easy recipe. Other than the rice, everything goes into the pot at the same time, so as Ron Popeil would say, "Set it and forget it." The only thing you'll really have to pay attention to is the rice, because depending on how much liquid is in your pot when you put it in (juice from the meat and the canned tomatoes can differ), the rice cooking time will vary. SERVES 6 TO 8

1 pound ground sirloin

½ teaspoon chili powder

1 teaspoon cayenne pepper

1 large white onion, chopped

3 cloves garlic, minced

1 medium head green cabbage, chopped

¼ cup cider vinegar

⅛ cup Worcestershire sauce

1 (28 ounce) can diced tomatoes, with juices

Salt and pepper

1 cup instant rice

In a large pot over high heat, add the ingredients in this order: sirloin, chili powder, cayenne pepper, onions, garlic, cabbage, cider vinegar, Worcestershire sauce, and tomatoes. Do not mix for 3 to 5 minutes, or until the beef is brown. When the beef is cooked, stir thoroughly, cover, and reduce the heat to low. Let simmer for 30 to 35 minutes.

Uncover, stir, and salt and pepper to taste. Add the instant rice, stir, and cover again. Depending on your rice, it will take 10 to 20 minutes to cook through.

When the rice is cooked, salt and pepper again, if needed, and serve.

Tips for Throwing Your Own Fabulous Casserole Party

Once you've mastered a few new recipes, you're going to want to show off your newfound casserole baking skills. Have some people over for a friendly, yet fierce, competition. Here are some tips to get you started.

Make your casserole party a competition.

Potlucks are fun, but people like to compete, especially when it comes to food, and even more so when it comes to perfecting and showing off a family recipe. If there's something at stake, even just a title, people are more likely to RSVP and show up.

Be strict.

Believe it or not, the more strict you are with your rules, the more people will get excited. People like to feel like they're part of something very official and organized. For the first two years, I had my casserole party in my apartment and competitors were only allowed through the doors in teams of two. If they wanted to bring a third person, they needed to bring a second casserole.

But be forgiving.

Upon hearing of the Annual Casserole Party, a few people emailed begging me to let them in. One didn't have time to cook, another was afraid. This worked out well because I was too broke to buy drinks, so beer and wine was their admission.

Have some kind of official system for judging.

Whether you write out ballots on index cards that go into a hat, or assign a few noncompetitors to judge, make the selection official. Lay out the criteria for judging in the original invitation and state it again before the party starts. Will you have a vegetarian category? Savory and non-savory? Is crust important? People want to know why they win, and why they lose. I added a "comments" section on my ballot cards and we had a fun time reading them at the end of the party.

Give fun prizes.

I think I had about twenty dollars in my bank account the year of my First Annual Casserole Party, and most of that went to the ingredients for my dish. But I dug through the silly gifts my dad had sent in my most recent care package from Missouri, hit up the Salvation Army for the funniest book I could find (a hardcover copy of *The Art of Sexual Magic*), and a 99-cent store for a knockoff Veggie Tales DVD and wreaths to "crown" the winners. People love getting prizes, no matter how ridiculous they are. By my Third Annual Casserole Party, a local independent kitchen store (the Brooklyn Kitchen) and Le Creuset sponsored the prizes.

Have fun.

You're the host(ess), so winning shouldn't be your first priority. Experiment with a new dish or make something you know no one else will bring. Whatever you do, hand out breath mints at the end of the night—because you know you're going to get at least three tuna noodle entries.

Mom, thanks for all the green bean casserole when I was a kid and for allowing me the freedom to be so industrious when I was a teenager. Dad and Pat, thanks for the monthly shipments of cookbooks and vintage Pyrex dishes and, thanks, Dad, for driving the U-Haul to New York even though I know you didn't really want to.

Thanks to Aunt Susie, for my casserole starter kit, and to my big sister, Heather, for being the first to introduce me to the wonderful combination that is cheddar cheese and sweet corn.

Stacey Sherman and Amanda Katz, thank you so much for encouraging me to write this book. Maria Flores and Pearl Cohen, you were great *sous*-chefs. Brian Fairbanks, thanks for always being so willing to try even the scarier-looking dishes. Thanks to Ruth Graham for being the first to write about the Annual Casserole Party and for being my friend and cheerleader for so many years.

Everyone who contributed or helped me track down a recipe: I owe you a drink, or seven. Special thanks to those who let me experiment on them (you know who you are), and to Brad Hewitt, Tom Riccobono, and Ben Young for testing recipes.

Thanks to Taylor Erkkinen at the Brooklyn Kitchen and all the wonderful people at Brooklyn Label, and even to American Apparel, for having so many stretchy pants readily available when I needed them most.

Thanks also to David Middleton, Jordana Rothman, Amy Wu, Julie Powell, Liz and Carol Nebiolo, Christine Onorati, Rachel Jones, Tessa Blake, Camille Becerra, Kristen Day, Adam Roberts, and the Food Network's Miriam Garron.

To my agent, Michael Bourret, thanks for being excited for me even when I was too tired to be excited for myself. And thanks to my editor, Meg Leder, who put up with me turning absolutely everything in very late and my not-always-so-detail-oriented mind. This book would not be here today without the wonderful people at Tekserve, who rescued my manuscript from my dying hard drive six days before it was due.

Most of all, thanks to my little sister and best friend, Jo, for being my biggest fan and having the guts to tell me when I need to shut up. If I could come up with something just as effective but less cheesy than "you are the wind beneath my wings," I would.

A Missouri native, **Emily Farris** grew up eating casseroles. After moving to New York City in 2000, she began to make her own, and learned that her mother's green bean casserole was, in fact, not her mother's—it was the Durkee Onion recipe. Since this devastating revelation, she has committed her life to creating and discovering original casserole recipes, and her Annual Casserole Party has been featured in the *New York Sun*, *New York Post*, and *Time Out New York*, and on Gawker.com.

When not slaving over casseroles in her tiny kitchen, Emily is a freelance writer and edits Nerve.com's culture blog, "Scanner." Her work has appeared in the *New York Sun*, the *Kansas City Star*, *Women's Wear Daily*, and the *Brooklyn Paper*, as well as numerous publications and websites most Americans have never heard of, including her own blogs at www.eefers.com and www.casserolecrazy.com. In the summertime, Emily teaches journalism and food writing at BEAM Camp, a camp for the fine and manual arts in New Hampshire.

Emily lives in Greenpoint, Brooklyn, with her cat, Eve. Comparisons to Rachael Ray are highly discouraged and may result in violent outbursts.